7 Lessons in Leadership
Master the Basics of Leading in 7 Steps

Dr Carol O'Connor

Material previously published in 2020 in *The Ultimate Leadership Book* and 2012, 2016 as *Leadership in a Week*.

First published in Great Britain by John Murray Business in 2020
An imprint of John Murray Press

This paperback 2nd edition published in 2026.

1

Copyright © Carol O'Connor 2012, 2016, 2020, 2026

The right of Carol O'Connor to be identified as the Author of the Work has been asserted by her in accordance with the Copyright, Designs and Patents Act 1988.

All rights reserved. No part of this publication may be reproduced, stored in a retrieval system, or transmitted, in any form or by any means without the prior written permission of the publisher, nor be otherwise circulated in any form of binding or cover other than that in which it is published and without a similar condition being imposed on the subsequent purchaser.

A CIP catalogue record for this title is available from the British Library

Paperback ISBN 9781399830119
ebook ISBN 9781399830126

Typeset by KnowledgeWorks Global Ltd.

Printed and bound in Great Britain by Clays Ltd, Elcograf S.p.A.

John Murray Press policy is to use papers that are natural, renewable and recyclable products and made from wood grown in sustainable forests. The logging and manufacturing processes are expected to conform to the environmental regulations of the country of origin.

John Murray Press
Carmelite House
50 Victoria Embankment
London EC4Y 0DZ

John Murray Business
Hachette Book Group
123 South Broad Street
Ste 2750
Philadelphia, PA 19109, USA

www.johnmurraybusiness.com

John Murray Press, part of Hodder & Stoughton Limited
An Hachette UK company

The authorised representative in the EEA is Hachette Ireland, 8 Castlecourt Centre, Dublin 15, D15 XTP3, Ireland (email: info@hbgi.ie)

Contents

Introduction   1

Lesson 1   2
  Self-awareness

Lesson 2   16
  Understanding people

Lesson 3   30
  Communication

Lesson 4   46
  Authority and power

Lesson 5   60
  Making decisions

Lesson 6   76
  Connecting and linking

Lesson 7   90
  Vision and inspiration

7 × 7   102

Further reading and information   107

Answers   108

About the author   108

Introduction

World events in business and politics reveal the importance of leadership. When it is absent, things fall apart. When it inspires, things improve. The purpose of this book is to encourage good people to become leaders by presenting the basics. Using a step-by-step approach, it shows the way to gain skill through training and effort.

Anyone can be a leader, even if modesty, lack of experience or self-doubt get in the way. This book guides readers to identify their strengths and build upon them. It also helps them to focus on their weaknesses in order to manage them better.

The central theme is **self-awareness.** Its importance underlies every activity, idea and suggestion. People often surprise themselves when they begin to explore their inner resources and discover that they have untapped leadership qualities. The result is personal growth as well as their leadership development.

However, taking charge is never easy. Each lesson in this book features the challenges as well as the benefits of leadership. Among these is the need to inspire other people and gain their support. Leaders must also set priorities, give direction and make decisions, often under pressure of both time and resources.

LESSON 1

Self-awareness

The first step to successful leadership is developing **self-awareness**. Leaders who lack personal insight are like tone-deaf musicians. Even if they gain technical skills through drill and practice, they begin each performance at a great disadvantage. They don't know if the notes they play are sweet or sour until their audience reacts.

Leaders need to cut the risk of striking the wrong note by adjusting their actions immediately. Self-awareness shows them how. Four topics support developing awareness:

- Leadership essentials
- Assessing strengths and weaknesses
- Following the leader
- Personal development.

Leadership essentials

There are three commonly held ideas about leadership:

1 Leadership is hereditary, and leaders are born to their role.
2 Character traits make a leader, including ambition, charisma, confidence, intelligence, initiative and independence, among many others.
3 Leaders emerge when special situations require them to accept leadership responsibility.

For many years, businesses, universities and the military have all debated the true nature of leadership. These ideas are still discussed around the world, and each idea has such firm support that this discussion could go on for ever.

However, everyone does agree on one point. It is clear that leaders must have the **support of their followers** because only this gives them the authority to act. When leaders lose this support, it is only a matter of time before they also lose their position as leader.

James MacGregor Burns wrote in the 1970s that leaders and followers need each other. He said that, when leaders represent their followers fairly, and followers loyally support their leaders, they create a virtuous circle. Also, if leaders later fail to respect their followers, then this circle breaks down, and the followers withdraw their support.

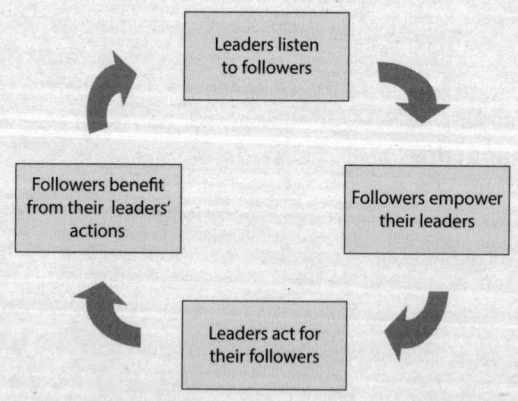

The virtuous circle of leadership

Respect is earned, and a leader's primary task is to convince people that they are worthy of receiving their support. Without followers, leadership exists only in the imagination of the would-be leader. The relationship between leaders and followers is crucial and far more important than birthright, personal qualities, a specific situation or any combination of these.

Any definition of leadership should include the idea of both leaders and followers needing each other. Here is a good definition:

> *'Leadership is the ability to present a vision so that others want to achieve it. Leaders need the skill to work with other people as well as the belief that they can make a difference.'*

People who have different backgrounds can work well together when they have a common purpose and shared goals. It's the leader's task to:

- focus everyone's attention on identifying these goals
- encourage discussion and debate until the goals are fully understood by all
- inspire action so that the goals are achieved.

All of this takes self-confidence and many would-be leaders have doubts about their abilities. There are many quiet heroes who question their own leadership ability but choose to accept responsibility anyway. This means they face self-doubt and then find the necessary confidence to take action. Therefore a first step towards leadership excellence is to gain **confidence.**

It's interesting that those who already believe in themselves and their own inner worth seem naturally to receive respect and recognition from others, while those who need to develop a sense of self-worth often receive little approval from others.

The process of gaining **respect** can begin in everyday life, when potential leaders make an effort to understand other peoples' difficulties. Mutual appreciation begins when colleagues notice other people's problems as well as their own. This is the basis for giving and receiving respect.

There are leaders who gain power through bullying or manipulation. History and news stories about politics and business show repeatedly that this kind of behaviour works for the short term only.

Those leaders who inspire, build, create and encourage others to succeed have **long-term success** and are remembered well into the future. Those who undermine, destroy, cheat and belittle others are avoided or destroyed as soon as their power weakens – as it always does.

Assessing strengths and weaknesses

Leaders need to know their strengths and weaknesses. This gives them a starting point to improve their leadership performance. One source of information about leadership effectiveness is **feedback** from other people. Asking colleagues what they think can be a valuable exercise. Occasionally, however, other people's ideas are biased, imprecise or lack perception.

So how can leaders know which comments are going to be helpful and which are not? Also, how can they avoid being defensive when they hear negative comments? They only make things worse if they try to explain away their behaviour or make excuses for themselves. They can also resent those who risked making a candid remark.

A good solution for dealing with negative comments is for leaders first to assess their own behaviour before asking anyone else for feedback. This **self-assessment** gives them a baseline against which their colleagues' comments can be considered carefully.

An honest self-image, clear goals for personal development and newly set performance standards can help a leader to decide whether colleagues' comments are helpful and appropriate, or signal the need for a further change of behaviour.

Self-assessment requires strict honesty. It is a waste of time and opportunity to create a fictional self-image. It is also self-defeating. Leaders need to see the difference between who they are now and who they want to be. They need to distinguish between their **current skills** and their **future hopes.** Honest self-assessment can produce goals for personal development and a plan of action to achieve them. Questions they can ask themselves include:

- Am I fair?
- Do I take responsibility?
- Do I listen?
- Do I care about other people?
- Am I honest?
- Am I willing to debate?
- Do my colleagues trust me?

Following the leader

Improved leadership is based on a careful study of **actual** behaviour. The first challenge is to ask: Would I follow a leader like myself? If not, then this is the starting point for discovering how to become the kind of leader that people want to follow.

It helps to think of a recent leadership experience and then focus on its details. Begin the process by **listing five positive and five negative examples** of your own actual and current leadership behaviour.

If there are fewer than ten examples, or if there are more positive than negative examples, this can signal a need for developing greater self-awareness. Concentrate and try to add one more example to each category before attempting the activity below.

However, fewer than ten examples could also mean a lack of leadership experience. If this is the case, then use the shorter list. After finishing the whole book, return to this section and repeat this activity until there are at least ten items.

After identifying examples of positive and negative leadership behaviour, it's time to include colleagues' opinions and beliefs. This new list should include their *honest opinions* about your

leadership behaviour. However, if it really isn't possible to ask colleagues directly, think about their reactions to you. Try to see yourself through other people's eyes.

Once again, make two lists. The first should include **positive** comments made by colleagues about your leadership behaviour or an estimate of their opinion about you. The second should include their *negative* comments or a best guess for this.

The following activity uses both your self-assessed and colleagues' lists in order to improve self-awareness.

> **Activity**
>
> Compare the two lists: your *self-assessment* and your *colleagues' ideas*.
> - Are they the same throughout?
> - If not, what are the differences?
> - How can you increase your awareness of how other people see you?
> - How can you increase self-awareness of your own behaviour?

Personal development

Identifying positive and negative leadership behaviour supports self-improvement. However, **behavioural change** should always build on qualities that a leader already has so that changes enrich natural personality. Everyone has a unique blend of qualities, such as courage, patience, faith, ambition and honesty. It's the unique mixture of **core qualities** that are the source of leadership success.

When leaders identify and accept their core qualities, then they can draw on these with greater confidence. It also helps them to discover what other qualities they need but may lack. This **self-audit** is a good first step to improving their leadership performance in future.

For example, an inability to give clear directions is a negative leadership behaviour. But there are a variety of potential causes for this, including a lack of confidence or decision-making skills, or even a need for clearer thinking or determination.

Therefore the same problem of 'an inability to give clear directions' could require a *different* solution depending upon each person's blend of qualities and their personal make-up. Improved leadership depends upon discovering what causes the negative leadership behaviour.

Positive behaviour

So how can leaders discover what qualities they already have and what qualities they need to develop? The two lists of positive leadership behaviour you compiled earlier in this lesson offer a way to begin this process. Each item from the two lists can help you to identify **personal qualities.**

For example, a positive item could read: 'remained calm during a crisis'. This behaviour could result from a variety of qualities such as courage, steadiness and trust. The task is to identify the quality that is the source of *remaining calm during a crisis*. When leaders know which qualities they already possess, they can actively draw upon them when the occasion requires it.

This insight has the direct benefit of improving self-confidence. 'I am calm in a crisis because I have courage' is a thought that obviously enhances self-image. Once a quality is identified for each item on the list, this can be written next to the item. Some qualities may be repeated and some may offer a surprise. The point of this activity is to discover qualities that underlie each example of positive behaviour.

This can be challenging if any qualities on the list are not normally associated with leadership, such as gentleness or humility. As a result, it can be tempting to ignore these qualities. However, many great leaders are guided by qualities like these and they are valuable features of any leader's personality. The challenge is learning how and when to express the less obvious leadership qualities so that they enhance leadership behaviour.

This is always possible, and the process begins with self-acceptance and the wish to discover how to express each quality in a strong and positive way. Personal development means **building on existing strengths** and **managing any weaknesses.** Masking or hiding personal qualities creates good actors, not good leaders.

Negative behaviour

The two lists of **negative leadership behaviour** you compiled earlier also offer learning opportunities. For example, if a comment on the list refers to using humour when presenting official company business, this creates an opportunity for choice, including:

- deciding that humour is an inappropriate leadership quality
- ignoring any criticism by showing increased clowning behaviour
- learning from the comment and deciding when, where and how a leader should use humour.

Rather than react blindly to negative comments, the leader can *analyse* them instead. On hearing a negative comment, a leader should ask the following questions.

- Did I really do what this person says I did?
- Does this person have all the facts?
- On reflection, do I truly believe that my behaviour was appropriate to all three essentials: time, place and audience?
- If not, when, where and how is it appropriate to express this quality in this way?

Changing behaviour

Both positive and negative feedback helps leaders see how their behaviour has an impact on other people. Positive comments are useful for identifying personal qualities. Negative feedback offers an opportunity to change behaviour.

In general, personal development can be organized into three areas: skills, knowledge and experience. Both positive and negative behaviour can offer ideas for improvement. It may help to review the lists of behaviour you compiled once again, both positive and negative. Choose just one item and decide *three* goals for that item:

1 a goal for developing a **new skill**
2 a goal for gaining **new knowledge**
3 a goal for having **new experience.**

After achieving all of the goals for that item, proceed to choose another item from the lists. Set three goals for that item to improve skills, knowledge and experience.

Solutions for self-doubt

Self-awareness supports leadership because it shows what skills and qualities can be developed. Here are examples of issues, both physical and emotional, that many people argue make them unfit to lead. If this is what they truly believe, then so be it. But if they feel even a small flicker of a wish to lead and to make a difference as a leader, then they should explore this.

They may discover that there is an antidote to resolve the issue that they believe is holding them back. In fact, there is always an antidote. There is always a way forward. There is always a solution. *Always.* The leader's job is to find it.

Issue	Solution
High, squeaky voice	Singing lessons
Confused thinking	Learn to play chess
Weak physical presence	Martial arts or fencing
Poor stamina	Swimming
Fear of public speaking	Join Toastmasters™
Indecisiveness	Video gaming

Summary

Self-awareness is the single most important leadership quality. Leaders need to examine their behaviour regularly to continue their growth and improve their self-knowledge.

Here is a checklist to help you review your leadership performance during any work week.

1 What qualities did you express consistently throughout the week?
2 What attention did you give to creating positive relationships with your colleagues?
3 List three strengths in the way you dealt with your colleagues.
4 How can you build on these strengths next week?
5 List three weaknesses in the way you dealt with your colleagues.
6 What quality or qualities do you need to develop in order to improve on these weaknesses?

Fact-check (answers at the back)

1. How should leaders react to negative comments?
a) By changing behaviour ❏
b) By ignoring them ❏
c) By analysing them ❏
d) By defending themselves ❏

2. What should be key to any definition of leadership?
a) Dignity ❏
b) Status ❏
c) Charisma ❏
d) Supporters ❏

3. What is the first step to assessing your strengths and weaknesses?
a) Ask a close friend ❏
b) Study yourself ❏
c) Ask your boss ❏
d) List future goals ❏

4. How is leadership improved?
a) With new skills ❏
b) With hope ❏
c) With ambition ❏
d) By adventures ❏

5. What is the most important thing leaders need?
a) Mentors ❏
b) Self-awareness ❏
c) Allies ❏
d) Risks ❏

6. What use is negative feedback?
a) To reveal enemies ❏
b) No use: it should be ignored ❏
c) To support development ❏
d) To punish people ❏

7. If someone feels unfit to lead, what should they do?
a) Find an antidote ❏
b) Give up ❏
c) Blame their boss ❏
d) Change jobs ❏

8. Confidence can be what?
a) Faked ❏
b) Developed ❏
c) Trouble ❏
d) The same as arrogance ❏

9. Which of their qualities should leaders know and build on?
a) The interesting ones ❏
b) The funny ones ❏
c) The worthy ones ❏
d) The core ones ❏

10. What kind of relationships do leaders need with their supporters?
a) Positive ❏
b) Temporary ❏
c) Complex ❏
d) Difficult ❏

LESSON 2
Understanding people

Leaders can use a one-size-fits-all approach only if everyone is actually the same size, and this is never going to be the case. There are as many different personalities in the world as there are people.

It's this diversity that makes life interesting. It generates new ideas and lively debate. Leaders who can attract a wide range of people enrich their business. However, they also need to understand people and be able to allow them to be different.

And it's an acceptance of differences that makes relationships strong. This lesson includes three topics that help leaders understand people better. They are:

- motivation and drives
- what people need
- rewards and values.

Motivation and drives

Leaders who recognize that everyone is different can encourage other people to be themselves and express their individual skills and qualities. This produces better work in the long term, although it may cause short-term frustration and frazzled tempers. It takes time to develop understanding when people are very different, but it is well worth the effort.

Fearful leaders try to squash individual difference, often because they are either unwilling or unable to understand those who are unlike themselves. This behaviour is unfortunate because these leaders lose an opportunity to see the world through other people's eyes. This insight could draw new customers or create new products or innovative services.

Although everyone is different, everyone is also the same. Scientific research says that, around the world and across cultures, people are motivated by the same things and in the same way. Motivation is like an internal engine driving people to get up in the morning, have breakfast and start their day's activities.

However, motivation works in two different ways. Some people are motivated only when they feel pressure from outside themselves to take action. An example would be a person who dislikes their job but needs the money that work provides. This is called **external motivation**, and the need for money is one example of an external motivator.

Other people get satisfaction from their jobs and enjoy going to work. Of course, they want and need to be paid, but their motivation comes from inside themselves. This is called **internal motivation.** Getting things done takes much less energy when motivation comes from within.

There will always be occasions when the pressure to achieve a goal or do a task comes from outside. When this happens, there's the risk of unwilling workers needing to be prodded and pushed, or reluctant leaders who grouch at everyone and are very difficult to follow.

However, each person can choose to control how they react to bad news or unpleasant work. People who make a habit of being internally motivated also give themselves the option of seeing unpleasant work as part of their own bigger plan. They will see themselves as the choosers, even when circumstances seemingly force them to accept.

> **Activity**
>
> 1 Make a list of all the things you really enjoy doing. Include hobbies, social and sports events, experiences of art, religion or nature and more. Very likely, you are *internally motivated* to do these things.
>
> 2 Make a list of all the things you do not like doing but know you must do anyway. Identify why you feel you must do these. Very likely, you are *externally motivated* to do these things.

At times, pressure from outside increases so gradually that leaders fail to see it happening. To avoid a sudden feeling of being overwhelmed or burned out, it's best to check daily on personal reactions to work and to colleagues. The outside pressure will still be there, but taking its measure allows people to pace themselves.

Leaders have to **ask what other people need,** and not assume that they know what is best for them without asking. Everyone needs different things at each stage of their lives. For example, a young person of 20 has different priorities and family needs from someone of 50. Also, what a middle-aged boss needs in terms of working hours, salary or holiday time may be very different from the junior manager who wants to travel or have a busy social life.

What people need

Abraham Maslow, a leading psychologist in the twentieth century, pioneered the study of healthy motivation. He said that people have five levels of need. The first level is the need to survive, the second level is the need to feel safe and secure, the third is the need to belong, the fourth is the need to be respected, and at the top is the need to have a sense of purpose.

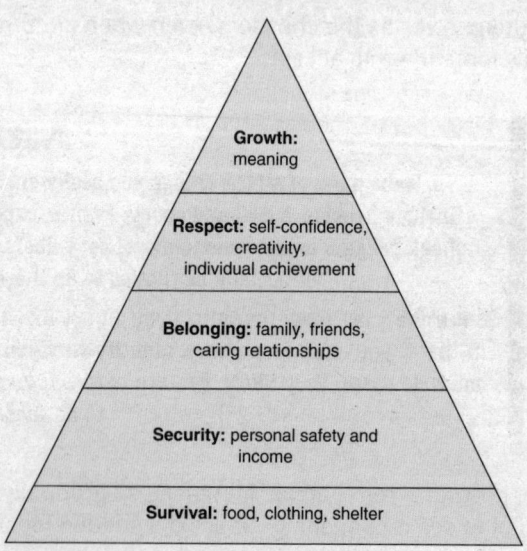

The 'Hierarchy of Needs', according to Abraham Maslow

Maslow defined each need as follows:

- **survival** – the drive to stay alive
- **security** – the need for stability, health and safety
- **belonging** – the wish to feel part of the social group
- **respect** – the need to be valued and respected
- **growth** – the need for purpose and meaning in life.

He said that satisfaction at each level allows a person to move naturally to the next level. For example, an infant is entirely dependent upon others for food, warmth and protection – that is, its survival. When this need is fulfilled, the infant must ensure that its next level of need is also fulfilled – that is, that its survival carries forward to the next day and then the next.

Babies learn at an early age how to get the attention they need: some scream while others smile and babble. Whatever tactic they use, their aim is first for survival and then security. When these needs are met, they are then able to relax into caring relationships. This is the level of belonging, and it is here that they discover who deserves their affection and how this should be shown.

Children who in their early years are denied safety and security may get stuck at this level. Their lack of family life, a secure home or a caring group may block their ability to fulfil their need to belong. If this happens, then in later life they will rarely feel fully relaxed in a social group. They are always on the lookout for danger and as a result question other people's motives.

This is because their attention is still on their need to satisfy survival and security needs. Even when they already have enough money, a home and a good job, they feel that something is missing and that they never have enough. Their pursuit of security can even get in the way of happy and healthy relationships.

Alternatively, when people are able to satisfy the first two levels of need, survival and security, they naturally focus on finding their place in the group. Even when rejected, their sense of security helps them to accept this so that they either find another group or try again to join the same group. They tend to see social rejection as a relatively minor issue.

According to Dr Maslow, healthy growth is based on satisfying each level of need in turn. Therefore, when the first three levels of need are satisfied, people naturally move to the two higher needs – that is, gaining respect and having a purpose and meaning in life.

Essentially, this means that people who are hungry and homeless always want to satisfy survival and safety needs before they feel ready to discuss philosophy. This also means that unsatisfied needs dominate behaviour. People who are under stress about money or are in poor health have less energy for team relationships.

Although business leaders are not expected to be psychologists, the **Hierarchy of Needs** is a valuable tool for understanding what motivates other people as well as themselves. They can ask if there are special circumstances influencing their colleagues. Even if they cannot help, their interest will have a positive effect.

Leaders should recognize the **impact of needs on motivation and performance.** This is the key to playing to people's strengths and also helping them to overcome their weaknesses. Motivation is never uniform or consistent within a group of people. Leaders can discover each person's starting point and build on this.

Leaders who want to support motivation can start by learning more about where their colleagues are blocked on the hierarchy. Whenever someone shows consistent frustration or anger about a level of need, this may mean they are fixed on satisfying the needs of the level below it.

That level may have trapped them so that they just can't understand the level above. Understanding people's frustration and limitations shows a leader **how to present a vision so that others want to achieve it.**

> ### Activity
> Think of a colleague at work.
> What does this person talk about most often:
> - physical comforts?
> - job security?
> - money and spending habits?
> - friends, family, social events?
> - job satisfaction, status, recognition?
> - values, principles, quality work?
>
> Are there any needs that they never discuss? What are they?
>
> Are there any needs that cause them to show impatience or anger when mentioned?

For example, when presenting an idea for a quality improvement programme – this is a level-four or -five need – to people who fear losing their jobs, it is less effective to talk about quality for its own sake. Describe instead what is in it for them and their job security.

Rewards and values

Some scientists say there are **three basic personality types** that result in three different kinds of behaviour. These can be summarized as:

1 ambitious and assertive
2 analytical and cautious
3 caring and supportive.

However, a person who is ambitious and assertive can also be caring, supportive, analytical or cautious whenever they make that choice or when the occasion requires it. Leaders with self-awareness widen their range of choice. When people think clearly about what they are doing, they will be more effective at achieving their goals.

These personality types are like habits. For example, when people are faced with similar choices every day, they develop a routine and habitual way of choosing what they do. Leaders can improve their performance by:

- identifying their personality type
- becoming aware of any habits and routines that limit their choices.

Ambitious and assertive

Ambitious and assertive types often have more ideas than there are hours in the day to achieve them. They are driven by a need to make their mark on the world and to influence other people. They very much dislike being ignored or refused access to important events and people.

Unsurprisingly, they like to be rewarded for their efforts. They want to be paid well, but primarily because this symbolizes their status. They also feel well rewarded by a large workspace or if they are praised often in public.

Although this type of person is very challenging for leaders, nothing stops this type when they are motivated to complete a task. It's also interesting that ambitious and assertive types don't mind being criticized. They have a rhinoceros hide. Instead of being hurt or embarrassed, they very likely will defend themselves or treat the criticism as a joke. Confident leaders who can accept debate are able to draw the best out of this kind of person.

Analytical and cautious

This personality type is committed to problem solving for its own sake. They are happiest when working alone and enjoy the solitude, the opportunity to concentrate, and the independence this gives them. Completing a task for them is very rewarding. For example, this kind of person genuinely feels burdened when expected to attend an office party because it interferes with their work.

Keeping their eyes down, they focus exclusively on what they are doing. They can be a big asset to the group because they bring depth to problem solving and enjoy studying complex issues.

However, the leader must be aware of this type's need for privacy. They are not shy; they just like to be alone and dislike offers of help from a caring and supportive type. They also resent the demanding behaviour of the ambitious and assertive type.

Caring and supportive

This personality type is happiest when offering care and support, and is naturally warm and friendly to all. Such people are a positive force in any group because they consider the needs of others and are generous and kind.

They feel most rewarded when their help is accepted. These are genuine virtues, but occasionally their support arises from a desire to please and be liked.

The leader's task is to guide this kind of person towards greater independence because too much people-focus can create deference to others when they should take more initiative.

Caring and supportive types can be intimidated by outspoken ambitious and assertive types because they interpret direct and bold feedback as harsh criticism. They also will need reassurance when analytical and cautious types, the loners in the group, refuse their support or even tell them to go away.

Activity

1. Using the list that follows, create a 'bank' of positive and negative words that you believe apply to yourself.

   Also, create another list of any words you've heard others say more than twice in relation to yourself.

   Do the words you circled show an obvious preference for one of the three kinds of behaviour?

2. Look at the descriptions of the three personality types. Do any of these descriptions match your behaviour?

   Do you have any habits that could get in the way of your ability to lead? What are they?

   Can you imagine what it would be like to be a different personality type?

Ambitious and assertive	
Positive features	*Negative features*
● confident	● arrogant
● dynamic	● pushy
● risk-taking	● gambling
● spontaneous	● impulsive
● directing	● dictatorial
● entrepreneurial	● unco-operative
● resourceful	● calculating
Caring and supportive	
Positive features	*Negative features*
● sensitive	● highly strung
● devoted	● doormat
● idealistic	● deluded
● friendly	● naive
● tolerant	● blind
● patient	● passive
● understanding	● submissive

Analytical and cautious	
Positive features	*Negative features*
● practical	● narrow-minded
● independent	● self-serving
● fair	● impersonal
● thorough	● obsessive
● reserved	● isolated
● methodical	● slow
● principled	● rigid

There are leaders who believe they need to appear special, more brilliant and somehow better than others. Even 50 years ago this would have been considered conventional leadership behaviour. However, this approach doesn't really work any more. People are better educated and more confident about asking questions and checking facts. The Internet, social networking, Twitter-type communication and blogging make information instantly available. As a result, leaders need real skill to inspire others.

Leaders who are willing to ask people what they value and then listen to the answers are likely to gain their attention. **Understanding other people** can lead to being better understood in turn.

Activity

Think of one occasion during the day when you took the lead.

Describe this occasion in one or two sentences. Then answer the following questions:

- What did you want to achieve as leader?
- What personal needs did you satisfy by leading?
- Were you aware of what motivated the people you were leading?
- Did you consider their needs?
- Was your behaviour 'ambitious and assertive', 'analytical and cautious' or 'caring and supportive'?

Summary

Successful leaders speak directly to people's needs, hopes and dreams. Recognizing and respecting these will create bonds of loyalty and trust between leaders and followers. It's also important to know what motivates people and what makes them feel rewarded.

Here is a checklist as a reminder that understanding people is a lifelong task. Use it to review leadership behaviour at the end of this book and also in the future.

1 Were you able to identify with your colleagues during the week?
2 How did people react when you asked them to do something or give you something?
3 Have any of the people you met merged into an indistinct group?
4 If you had taken time, could you have learned more about other people this week?
5 List three of your strengths for the way you learn about other people.
6 How can you build on these strengths?
7 List three weaknesses in the way you learn about other people.
8 What behaviour do you need to change to improve on these weaknesses?

Fact-check (answers at the back)

1. What are externally motivated people driven by?
   a) Outside pressure ❏
   b) Information ❏
   c) Gossip ❏
   d) Changes in the weather ❏

2. What are internally motivated people driven by?
   a) Power ❏
   b) Friendship ❏
   c) Choice ❏
   d) Money ❏

3. Which of the following is *not* included in Dr Maslow's hierarchy?
   a) Growth ❏
   b) Power ❏
   c) Survival ❏
   d) Security ❏

4. When colleagues are afraid of taking risks, what should you do?
   a) Ignore them ❏
   b) Ridicule them ❏
   c) Force them ❏
   d) Respect them ❏

5. What has an impact on motivation?
   a) Family ❏
   b) Fulfilling needs ❏
   c) Travel ❏
   d) Education ❏

6. Which of the following do ambitious and assertive types want?
   a) Influence ❏
   b) Isolation ❏
   c) Affection ❏
   d) Fairness ❏

7. Which of the following do caring and supportive types want?
   a) Caution ❏
   b) Arguments ❏
   c) Harmony ❏
   d) Power ❏

8. Which of the following do analytical and cautious types want?
   a) To take risks ❏
   b) Privacy ❏
   c) Teamwork ❏
   d) Friendship ❏

9. How can you demotivate ambitious and assertive types?
   a) With a high salary ❏
   b) With a big office ❏
   c) With anger ❏
   d) By neglect ❏

10. How can you demotivate caring and supportive types?
    a) With criticism ❏
    b) With parties ❏
    c) With friendship ❏
    d) With praise ❏

LESSON 3

Communication

Communication is the glue that holds people together. It's the way they share ideas and feelings, and the means they use to bond and form groups. Its importance is most obvious when it breaks down. Almost immediately, disagreements, quarrels and misunderstandings occur.

For all that, communication skills are frequently taken for granted. People assume that only time, effort and sincerity are necessary to communicate successfully. This optimistic view ignores the importance of emotion, motivation, intelligence, risk-taking and feelings of competition, among many other issues.

Therefore communication is the third step for improving leadership, and this lesson features the topics of:

- listening and speaking
- making an impression
- group discussion.

Listening and speaking

In its simplest form, communication is an exchange of information. This happens most often through speaking and listening, two activities that require complex skills and draw upon a person's lifetime of experience.

Even a brief encounter consisting of a casual greeting results from years of practice. Through trial and error, people create a personal style and adapt their behaviour to meet the changing needs of each situation. However, these exchanges happen so quickly and occur so often that people rarely consider whether they are any good at just saying hello.

It is important, however, for leaders to get this right because a greeting sets the tone of the exchange and shows the degree of respect that people share. The way a leader makes eye contact, gestures and chooses words invites people either to listen to the main portion of the conversation or, alternatively, turns them off.

Listening

This skill requires a leader to be aware of three things: bias, visual signs and vocal signals.

1 Bias Everyone's point of view includes some bias, even if this is not entirely conscious. Bias, by definition, is a way of thinking that colours a point of view about a person, an event or an idea. For leaders, bias can influence and even undermine the ability to understand and interpret what they see and hear. The main challenge is to identify when bias weakens judgement and reduces understanding about what is said.

Bias is a problem when it distorts understanding. It actually becomes dangerous when a leader doesn't know it is happening or even denies its existence. Bias can cause a leader to ignore essential data – for example, when the information source is unattractive or in some way different from the leader.

Indicators of bias include:

- extreme reactions to people or situations, either in favour or against
- paying attention only to that part of a presentation that is already understood
- assuming there is an understanding of what is being said even before a statement is finished.

2 Visual signs These refer to a speaker's gestures and movements, what is often called **body language.** There are numerous books, courses, podcasts and videos about this topic that interpret commonly used gestures and signs. These often are a sincere effort to improve understanding.

However, in a world that brings together different cultures through media and transportation links, leaders have to remind themselves constantly that gestures can mean different things to people from different societies.

This is because people interpret body language according to their own backgrounds. Any population including more than one nationality will lack a single meaning for hand gestures or facial expressions. So it's better to avoid thinking that there is only one meaning for body language as if there were a universal code available.

Gestures add a layer of meaning to what's being said with words. They enrich communication and alert a listener to subtleties within the message. For example, gestures and expressions show when the speaker is being funny, ironic, dramatic or sad, and a range of other emotions. They can also show intensity of feeling. Visual signs make it easier for listeners to understand what the speaker really means.

Emoticons are a substitute for physical gestures when speakers use the written word. These are icons showing facial expressions that are made using punctuation marks. When using instant messaging, email, text or online posts of any kind, emoticons show emotion and mood. Emoticons came into being in response to the increased dependence on electronic text-based communication. Their emergence recognizes that it's a mistake to assume automatically that people will understand a writer's intentions or feelings. They alert readers to be aware of emotional content whenever there may be room for doubt. Crucially, they serve to remove emotional ambiguity from whatever is being written.

3 Vocal signals Listening to the sound and tone of a speaker's voice improves understanding. Speakers can express their ideas and add deeper and richer meaning by raising and lowering the volume of their voice, changing its tone or pitch or by varying their speed of delivery. They can signal their emotional state as well as their attitude towards the audience through their voice.

At times, it's more important to hear these subtle, vocal messages than the content of what is being said. If a speaker's tone of voice contrasts with the content of their message, then it's necessary to ask for clarification. This requires tact, but it improves understanding.

Speaking

Some leaders like to let their words flow freely and their ideas emerge spontaneously without any internal editing. This is fine for the naturally eloquent, the vivid raconteur or the disciplined presenter. It also works for everyday conversation or lightweight social chat. However, if speakers suffer from confused thinking, ramble around their topic, or enjoy the sound of their own voice, then they have a problem.

A challenging business conversation requires an ordered and logical presentation of ideas. Leaders must also be aware of managing their time and respecting other people's. Clear and direct delivery encourages listening.

Effective speakers use three techniques to make listening easier. These are headlining, pacing and summarizing.

1 Headlining This is a brief opening statement that catches the listener's attention. It is comparable to a news headline that signals a story's main idea. Speakers can organize what they want to say in a series of headlines. This helps listeners identify the key points and also helps speakers avoid a rambling or wordy presentation.

Activity

During the day, observe three conversations between people you do not know.

Conversation 1: Bias

- If you joined this conversation, would you feel bias towards the other people?
- What would cause this bias?
- What could you do about your own bias in order to improve your ability to listen?

Conversation 2: Visual signals

- Do these people seem to have similar backgrounds?
- Do they use similar gestures and facial expressions?
- Do you understand their significance?
- How do you know that you understand?
- What could you do to improve your ability to understand these visual signals?

Conversations 3: Vocal signals

- Do both speakers use the same tone and volume?
- Do they seem aware of how their voices sound?
- If you joined this conversation, would you use a similar tone of voice and volume?
- What could you do to become more conscious of how your own voice affects other people?

2 Pacing Good speakers watch their audience and pace their delivery to meet their listeners' needs. This could mean that they pause to invite their listeners to comment. Their listeners can then answer the speaker or offer their own new headline. However, some speakers believe that their turn is over only once they have used up every one of their own ideas. This can exhaust an audience.

Pacing also refers to changing the speed of delivery as well as pausing before or after key ideas to create dramatic interest. An unwavering tone of voice and rhythm is often boring.

3 Summarizing 'I tell them what I plan to say; then I tell them; then I tell them what I just said.' This is an age-old saying for report writing and public speaking, but isn't really suitable for everyday conversation. It does contain a gem of wisdom, however.

Summarizing is a good way for speakers to end each topic by repeating the headline and then listing, bullet-point fashion, whatever has been discussed or agreed. The speaker then asks whether everyone understands.

Activity

During three conversations, practise these techniques.

Conversation 1: Headlining

- Before you begin speaking, think of headlines for your main thoughts.
- Begin by stating your first headline.
- Speak so that you expand only on this first headline.
- Move to the next headline after your listener responds.
- Be aware of when you move to the next headline.

Conversation 2: Pacing

- Listen carefully to the pace used by the other speaker.
- Then, when you speak, notice if your pace is different.
- If so, alter your pace to match that of the other person.
- Watch for signals that the other person has finished.
- Identify the signals you use to let others know you have finished speaking.

Conversation 3: Summarizing

- When you finish a headline, paraphrase what you said.
- After several contributions by both speakers, highlight the key points that were covered.
- When the discussion slows, clearly state the conclusions reached so far.
- At the end of the conversation, list all the headlines that were covered.

Making an impression

Communication also includes the impression people make. There are speakers who make an audience feel uneasy, and others who create a relaxed atmosphere. People may not know exactly why they trust someone or, alternatively, want to back away from someone else. They may just sense that something is wrong.

For example, there are those who smile with their mouths, but glare with their eyes. People notice and then decide not to trust that speaker. Another source of discomfort can be a mismatch with appearance. For example, a speaker wearing an expensive suit can raise alarm bells if listeners also see scuffed shoes, dirty hair and chewed fingernails.

The overall impression these speakers make is one of disharmony. This can be accidental and occur because speakers don't know that they are sending out contradictory signals. Their goal should be to use gestures, facial expressions, language and style of dress so that these are in harmony with the content of what they are saying. The six actions leaders can take to create a single and harmonious impression are:

1 have a goal
2 check your appearance
3 manage your emotions
4 choose time and place
5 keep it simple
6 control yourself.

Have a goal

A discussion is more satisfying when everyone believes time is well used, progress is being made and that learning is taking place. This is easier when there is a clear purpose for the communication. This purpose decides choice of words and brings confidence to their delivery.

Check your appearance

Look in the mirror and ask yourself: Would I trust or believe me? If the answer is no, then ask why. This often requires humility. Ensuring that style of dress matches the situation helps listeners accept what is being said.

Manage your emotions

Leaders need a delivery style that will work in a variety of situations. For example, when doctors give bad news to their patients, they know that this requires gravity and a serious manner. But consider the situation of the doctor who just moments before seeing a patient receives very good news.

Professionals train themselves to match their own facial expressions to the needs of the situation. To do this, they must know how they are feeling themselves and then keep this in check.

Choose time and place

This means planning when and where a message should be delivered. The question to ask before speaking is this: How would I react to hearing this information at this time and in this place? Whatever the answer, act in line with it.

Keep it simple

Decide the main points and phrase these into headlines. Avoid using leadership as an excuse to share your every thought and feeling. The task is to get a message across in a memorable, but simple, way.

Control yourself

This refers to self-discipline. For example, when people disagree or express their anger, stay calm at all times. Anyone can react emotionally or in a mindless way. Leaders should not.

Even if the situation seems to demand shouting, banging the desk or even running away, the leader stays calm. Why? Because that is part of the job of being leader.

Let's summarize:

> **Preparation for important communication**
> - What are your goals for this occasion, both personal and professional?
> - Will your style of dress, choice of language and tone of voice make a single harmonious impression?
> - Is the timing and choice of communication method the right one for delivering your message?
> - Are you as fully prepared to listen as well as speak?
> - What do you plan to learn from this experience in order to improve your impression in future?

Group discussion

It's the leader's responsibility to open a debate, encourage everyone to participate, and guide the discussion towards agreement. Group discussion, when managed well, supports unity and understanding. This can be a challenge when difficult issues are raised and there is little or no agreement at the start.

Some leaders give up at the first sign of dissent or confusion and order silence. They fear loss of control. This is a mistake. It's better not to open a debate or encourage people to share opinions if they are later told they may not disagree.

This is unwise for three reasons:

1 because people will express disagreement only when the leader is absent
2 because avoiding conflict makes a leader look weak and panic-stricken, not strong
3 because it is rude to ask for opinions and then change direction and say be quiet – colleagues are unlikely to share their opinions in future as a result.

It takes courage to listen to opposing views and also to insist that a debate is respectful to all. Leaders who are committed to creating understanding demonstrate this by setting a tone of tolerance to other people's views. It's already been said that respect generates respect, and the discussion leader has the power to begin this process.

The main challenges are to encourage **active participation** while avoiding an opinion free-for-all or allowing the group show-off to talk until everyone is asleep. Genuine unity emerges when differences are accepted. It helps when the group has ground rules to ensure that everyone gets a fair hearing. The leader can then maintain those rules.

When a group lacks ground rules, the leader has to get the group itself to create them. **Ground rules** should include: attentive listening, no interruptions, taking turns to speak, and waiting to be acknowledged before speaking.

Formal meetings may require using the organization's in-house guidelines or legal reporting standards. There are reference books describing how a meeting moderator should behave when leading formal meetings. This next section, however, offers ideas for leading *informal* discussions.

In informal discussions, leadership needs to have the skills of:

- guiding
- paraphrasing
- intervention.

Guiding

The first task for discussion leaders is to state the purpose of the discussion, the amount of time available and a reminder of the ground rules. Once the discussion is under way, the leader gently guides participants so that they stay on track, and ensures that no single person dominates the debate. In practice, this means that no one speaks until they are called upon to do so.

The leader must be scrupulously fair because people soon lose interest when some people take too long to make their point or when others are repeatedly called upon. The situation worsens when people begin talking over those who have been speaking for too long. If speaking in turn is a ground rule (and it should be), then it's the leader's job to maintain this.

It takes courage to insist that forceful people wait their turn because leaders become unpopular with those who like to dominate. Leaders have to be firm when anyone interrupts.

Their job is to point out that interruptions are not allowed and that everyone must wait their turn.

The leadership qualities that support effective group discussion include tact, a good memory for what's been said and who has spoken, a sense of humour, firmness and a commitment to timekeeping.

> **Helpful phrases**
>
> 'That's an interruption. Please allow the speaker to finish.'
>
> 'I've got to ask everyone not to interrupt.'
>
> 'Let each speaker have their say.'
>
> 'That's an interesting contribution but someone else is speaking. Please wait your turn.'
>
> 'Your enthusiasm is great, but we need to hear as many different views as time allows.'

Paraphrasing

When a discussion wanders from the main point, paraphrasing allows the leader to bring it back on track. This is achieved by summarizing what was said during the digression, and then linking it – if at all possible – back to the main discussion topic. This has to be done in a non-judgemental manner.

When leaders catch digression quickly, it's easier to reaffirm the main topic without obvious strain on people's time and attention. The person who began the digression can also be invited to add the topic to the next meeting's agenda.

> **Helpful phrases**
>
> 'This is interesting but we've left the main topic.'
>
> 'This covers some good points and they link to our main topic in this way.'
>
> 'Let's summarize this side topic's points so far. We can return to it later in this meeting or put it on the agenda for next time.'

Intervention

When two people are locked in a dispute, the leader has to intervene or their disagreement will dominate an entire meeting. This situation occurs most often when there are strong factions in a group. A spokesperson for one faction speaks forcefully and then the spokesperson for the opposition answers. It's just like a tennis match, but with a conversational ball going back and forth.

The leader must step in immediately and point out that two opinions have been presented, and now other members of the group should comment. If the same people ask to speak again, the leader has to insist that they've had their say and now others need a chance to speak.

> **Helpful phrases**
>
> 'Thanks for your views. Now, what do others in the group think?
>
> 'You two, please, take a back seat while someone who agrees with each of you paraphrases.'
>
> 'Let's avoid a dialogue between just two people. Who else wants to comment?'

Summary

Communication skills benefit all aspects of life, not just leadership development. Although they are often taken for granted, these skills are essential. Listening and speaking are foundation stones. Also important is the impression a leader makes. This can be managed by thinking about six actions to make a positive impression.

Here is a checklist to review communication behaviour:

1 How would you describe your communication behaviour during the past week?
2 What did you like and not like about this, and how can you improve?
3 Did you prepare for any important meetings by thinking about the impression you would make?
4 List three strengths for your listening skills. How can you build on these strengths?
5 List three weaknesses for your listening skills. How can you manage these weaknesses?
6 Now list three strengths for your speaking skills. How can you build on these strengths?
7 List three weaknesses for your speaking skills. How can you manage these weaknesses?
8 Did you lead a group discussion this week? If so, what did you like and not like about the way you led this?

Fact-check (answers at the back)

1. Which word best describes bias?
   a) Distortion
   b) Clarity
   c) Seeing
   d) Honesty

2. What are emoticons?
   a) Important speeches
   b) Football chants
   c) Radio signals
   d) Punctuation marks

3. What does a 'single and harmonious impression' lead to?
   a) Expensive clothes
   b) Good manners
   c) Trust
   d) A clearer voice

4. Which of these helps make a positive impression when speaking?
   a) Staring
   b) Forcefulness
   c) Ambition
   d) Timing

5. Which of these supports group discussion?
   a) Ground rules
   b) Dominant speakers
   c) Bias
   d) Emotion

6. When listening, which of these needs your attention?
   a) Content
   b) Bias
   c) Cleanliness
   d) Pacing

7. When speaking, what do gestures add?
   a) Confusion
   b) Sound
   c) Meaning
   d) Distance

8. When speaking, what do headlines signal?
   a) Urgency
   b) The core idea
   c) News
   d) Timing

9. What does paraphrasing help the leader manage?
   a) Anger
   b) Laziness
   c) Writing
   d) Digression

10. What does group discussion lead to?
    a) Unity
    b) Fear
    c) Wasted time
    d) Egotism

LESSON 4

Authority and power

For many people, the words 'authority' and 'power' are menacing and negative. This is because bad leaders from both history and recent times have made them their own. But there are many more leaders who have integrity than those who want the role for glory, power or to satisfy their greed.

The best leaders use authority and power wisely and have the confidence to encourage debate. Different opinions interest them and they can listen to others without feeling threatened. This lesson features five topics that support using authority and power effectively. They are:

- styles of leadership
- four kinds of power
- using power
- adapting to events
- delegation.

What is authority?

Having the title 'Leader' doesn't automatically mean that a person has the authority to lead. A job title is just the starting point. It is the leader's behaviour that encourages people to give their support or discourages them from doing so. In practice, appointed leaders can even be ignored or bypassed.

These are leaders in name only who believe that they must use threats or coercion to get people to obey them. This approach requires an enormous outlay of their energy. It would actually be much easier for them to behave in a way that inspires confidence and makes people want to follow. However, this does take skill.

Discussion, feedback sessions and debate are essential for leaders to learn what their followers want and need. Therefore part of a leader's job is to encourage this. Repressing, ignoring or discouraging different opinions in the group is the sign of a weak and frightened leader who is hiding behind a role in order to stay in control.

Here's a definition of authority:

> *'Authority is the legitimate and justified claim to exercise power. It is granted by others and can be based on a set of rules, established traditions, or the emerging needs of a situation.'*

Confidence, curiosity and **tolerance** are qualities of strong leadership. Inevitably, leaders who possess these also want to include other people in discussions. They willingly share the limelight whenever it is appropriate.

Every leader potentially can be undermined, manipulated or overthrown. However, this results more often when leaders refuse to allow other people to express different points of view. An open attitude and a willingness to listen create a bond between leader and follower. This is because people like those who listen to them and who show an interest in their ideas.

Styles of leadership

Authority is expressed through leadership style. Research shows that there are three basic styles. These are:

- democratic
- autocratic
- permissive.

Democratic

A democratic style is based on mutual respect among colleagues, regardless of role or status. When these leaders discover their colleagues lack skills or experience, they create opportunities for them to grow and develop. The strength of this style is the positive atmosphere it creates and the belief that innovation will be rewarded and new ideas tested and explored.

People learn from one another when leaders use this style, and everyone gains, including the leaders. There are few more satisfying leadership experiences than to start with a group of moderately skilled people who then work and grow together so that they emerge as a skilled and powerful team.

In contrast, there are leaders who feel frustrated because they believe themselves surrounded by witless underlings rather than peers. Even when they hire intelligent and talented new people, these new ones also gradually prove themselves unsatisfactory. These leaders have a serious problem because they cannot see that their leadership is to blame. When the whole world looks consistently wrong, it is time to improve the viewer – not the viewed.

Autocratic

During times of turbulence and chaos, the autocratic leadership style appeals to those who long for a strong boss who will to tell them what to do. Certainly, there are enough historic examples of dictators that were invited into power to show that autocratic leaders can be valued.

However, there is strong research which suggests that groups with a single, command-giving leader suffer poorer productivity over the long term, and are far less profitable than those that are democratically led.

When leaders are too frightened, too proud or too conceited to listen to their colleagues, they weaken their own authority. In contrast, it's a show of personal strength to open a discussion. It shows confidence in their authority, good judgement and their willingness to learn.

Permissive

The permissive style is often a misguided attempt at being democratic. These leaders are reluctant to impose their will on other people. This may result from a dislike of being bossed themselves, a lack of interest in their work, self-doubt or even laziness.

Whatever the reason for their refusal to take responsibility for leadership, these leaders are infuriating to other people whose work requires co-ordination, active support and direction.

People need and want a plain-speaking leader to remind them of their goals, keep them on track, focus their discussions, challenge performance and act as their champion. Permissive leaders fail to realize that this is part of their job.

Although colleagues may *like* these seemingly nice-guy leaders – both male and female – they also describe them as weak, spineless and incompetent, and regret the day they began working for them. Sadly, if or when these leaders discover what other people think about them, they are shocked, hurt and disappointed.

However, permissive leadership may be beneficial when leading highly creative people or those with professional or technical expertise. A leader using the permissive style allows these types of people to digress and explore while encouraging them to work together and produce results. This style depends on vision and sharing inspiring ideas on a regular basis.

All three leadership styles can both help and harm a situation and leaders need to decide when to use each style. We can sum this up as follows:

Benefits

Democratic: These leaders encourage everyone to use their skills and talents so that more work of a higher quality gets done.

Autocratic: These leaders offer speed, single-mindedness and clarity when firm direction is needed. There are occasions when people do gain from being told exactly what to do.

Permissive: These leaders are best when taking responsibility for highly creative people who flourish in a loosely structured environment. This style is useful when little co-ordination is needed.

Frustrations

Democratic: These leaders drive impatient colleagues crazy because discussion takes time and slows progress.

Autocratic: These leaders are so one-sided that they frustrate colleagues who want to contribute ideas and offer new information.

Permissive: These leaders force their colleagues to accept inactivity through their avoidance of giving direction and taking action themselves.

Four kinds of power

There are four kinds of power used in most organizations. Leaders can use all of them or just one. The four are:

1 designated
2 expert
3 charismatic
4 information.

Designated power

This kind of power is linked to a specific job or role. Leaders with this power are officially appointed to act on behalf of their organization. When leaders leave their role, they also give up the power that went with that role.

This means that the department head who vacates a position no longer has the power to lead that department. This power passes to the next person taking that role. Although a loss of role-related power can seem obvious, there are people who refuse to give it up or to accept that someone else has taken their former role. People create bad feeling when they refuse to step aside gracefully.

Expert power

This kind of power results from the personal talents, skills and experience of the people who possess it. They have this power regardless of the role they fill. When they move to another job, their expertise goes with them. This power is acquired through study, training and learning new skills.

When a person has both *designated* and *expert* power, they are in a very strong position. However, those who really enjoy the technical aspects of their work often find their designated role gets in the way of using their expertise. This causes some experts to avoid designated roles.

Expert power is often used informally. Leaders who have a designated role as their only source of power benefit everyone when they support the experts in the group.

Charismatic power

Those with charismatic power have both a blessing and a curse. They are frequently wild cards in an organization. Historically, the highly charismatic are those leaders who end up dead, in disgrace, alone, in prison or in Holly- or Bollywood.

Charismatic leaders can truly inspire their colleagues to do their best. The downside is that it is this very ability that can then tempt these leaders to depend upon charisma as their sole source of influence. This is less than wise. To ensure that they have substance along with charm and dazzle, these leaders should develop and draw upon other sources of power as well.

Information power

Digital technology enables storage of vast amounts of information. People who know how to organize data and then access it as usable knowledge are now crucial to organizations. Regardless of job title or placement within the hierarchy, knowledge workers are truly powerful.

In the past, it was the long-serving members of staff who had information power. They would be called upon to remember where items were stored, or when an event occurred. Databases replace human memory, and those managing the data now have this power.

Using power

Exercising authority is easier when the leader's source of power is obvious and easily recognized. Designated power is the only one that is given to a leader by others. Expert power results from study and experience. Charisma is an internal quality that attracts and fascinates other people. And information power, like expertise, is acquired and is based on data-management skills

On rare occasions, a leader has all four kinds of power. This strengthens their leadership position, but can also be dangerous because people avoid questioning them. These leaders risk surrounding themselves with yes-saying admirers. Although this can also happen to those with just one kind of power, it is more likely when a leader has several.

> **Activity**
>
> 1 Think of examples – one for each – of all four kinds of power that you have seen **other people** exhibit.
>
> 2 Think of occasions – one for each – when **you** have exhibited each kind of power.
>
> 3 Think of an occasion when you exhibited the wrong kind of power – e.g. you overwhelmed colleagues with data when your task was to lead a meeting.
>
> If you could relive this occasion, what would you do differently?
>
> What kind of power would you use instead?

Adapting to events

Effective leaders are flexible when deciding which leadership style is best at any given time. They do this by identifying the stage of development of their group. This is called the **Situational Leadership Model.** It says that groups develop in four stages, and that leaders should adapt their style to match the group's needs at each stage.

- The **first stage** starts when the group forms. The leader's role at this point should be directive to ensure that the work gets under way. This means telling people what to do at first to get things moving. Once group members understand their assignments, the leader encourages them.
- The **second stage** is coaching, where the leader explains why the task is important and supports group members to gain skill and confidence.
- The **third stage** encourages strong relationships so that group members can better support each other. This is the participating stage and the leader asks everyone to offer ideas and solutions to improve the task.
- At the **fourth stage,** the leader delegates work decisions to group members who take responsibility themselves for the work.

Groups that go through all four stages are said to be **mature.** This four-stage model helps leaders decide what leadership style best serves their group's needs. It also explains why groups on occasion benefit from being told what to do and at other times resent this same behaviour.

Delegation

Delegation skills help leaders move the group forward. They are particularly useful at the *coaching* and *participating* stages of development because delegation encourages group members to learn new skills and gain more experience. This supports their accepting more responsibility within the group. There are four steps to effective delegation:

1 define the task
2 explain why it is important
3 describe expectations
4 evaluate results when the task is finished.

1 Define the task

This step can seem so obvious that some leaders don't give it any attention. Instead, they hand out assignments and assume people will guess what is needed and by when. Leaders who want to ensure reliable results need to do two things:

- take time to decide what they want
- ask the person being delegated how they think the task should be done.

Asking to hear the delegatee's ideas at the very start reveals their level of knowledge and understanding. It also raises their level of interest and commitment to getting the job done. This is called **empowerment** because it encourages the person who will do the task to take responsibility for its completion and success.

2 Explain why it is important

Many people do their best when they know the purpose of a task. They want to see how it fits into their work overall and why it is important.

This information also makes their deadlines more meaningful and helps them set priorities, organize steps, and fit their work into what their colleagues are doing on the same project. This reduces mistakes and duplicated effort.

3 Describe expectations

People want to know what is expected of them; otherwise their work is a guessing game. This should include budget limits, quality standards and any required procedures or processes. Some leaders give delegatees little information of this kind, arguing that they want to give the delegatee complete freedom to decide what to do. However, their colleagues are not mind-readers. Unless they have done the same task before, the delegator should explain what is required.

Making colleagues guess also undermines motivation because they do not know where they stand. This is power hoarding and negative leadership behaviour. Even when a leader is rushed, under stress or has an optimistic belief in a colleague's abilities, expectations should be explained.

4 Evaluate results when the task is finished

This step builds on the previous one. Fully explained expectations give clear performance goals towards which everyone can work. Some leaders share criteria for success only after the task is complete. This often causes unnecessary disappointment when a task is evaluated. It's also unfair because guessing a goal and getting it right is almost impossible.

Activity
- Describe an episode during the day when you were a leader.
- What kind of power did you use?
- Could you have used any other kind(s) of power?
- Which style of leadership did you use? Were you happy with this choice?
- What stage of development would you estimate your group has achieved?

Summary

The best leaders want to take charge in order to make a positive impact on the world. This means they need to have both authority and power. This lesson focused on leaders being confident enough to invite challenges, questions and comments from other people.

Use the following checklist to review the way you use power now. You can also use these questions to examine your use of authority and power in future as well.

1 Do you feel good about how you express power and authority?

2 If yes, what do you like? If no, what do you dislike and how can you change this?

3 Are you aware of using different kinds of power?

4 Are you better at using one kind over the others?

5 Are you happy with your leadership style?

6 What do you like and not like about your style?

7 How can you improve?

Fact-check (answers at the back)

1. What is authority?
   a) Automatic ❑
   b) Power ❑
   c) Harmful ❑
   d) Threatening ❑

2. Which word refers to a kind of power?
   a) Expert ❑
   b) Dictator ❑
   c) Helpless ❑
   d) Absolute ❑

3. When is the permissive leadership style best?
   a) When people are frightened ❑
   b) When people are creative ❑
   c) When people are lazy ❑
   d) When people are focused ❑

4. When is the autocratic leadership style best?
   a) During discussion ❑
   b) During periods of inaction ❑
   c) During a debate ❑
   d) During a crisis ❑

5. Which is a step in the delegation process?
   a) Guessing ❑
   b) Awareness ❑
   c) Evaluation ❑
   d) Coaching ❑

6. What do democratic leaders want their colleagues to be?
   a) Strong ❑
   b) Obedient ❑
   c) Frightened ❑
   d) Silent ❑

7. What is charismatic power similar to?
   a) Aggression ❑
   b) Trouble ❑
   c) Resentment ❑
   d) Charm ❑

8. Democratic leaders frustrate people who are what?
   a) Attentive ❑
   b) Impatient ❑
   c) Debaters ❑
   d) Talented ❑

9. Autocratic leadership can lead to what?
   a) Peace ❑
   b) Freedom ❑
   c) Weakness ❑
   d) Success ❑

10. Which of the following is a stage in the Situational Leadership Model?
    a) Coaching ❑
    b) Expert ❑
    c) Designated ❑
    d) Information ❑

LESSON 5

Making decisions

There are two approaches to decision making: rational (step by step) and creative (intuition driven). Leaders who can draw on both approaches make better decisions.

This lesson, however, focuses on rational decision making. It is useful for leaders who are required to make fast decisions when under pressure. It also helps leaders develop their analytical skills, forcing them to think clearly when faced with a sea of information. The three core topics for rational decision making are:

- setting priorities
- clarifying goals
- a step-by-step method.

Setting priorities

Leaders often have to make several decisions at once and juggle different streams of information at the same time. They also suffer distraction when their decisions have an impact on other matters. When this happens, they need to identify just how much interdependence exists across a variety of issues.

Setting priorities is therefore an essential skill. This takes discipline because some decisions demand attention even though they lack genuine urgency or importance. Alternatively, other truly vital matters can be ignored because they lack glamour or a noisy advocate pressing for their attention.

The first step is to recognize that there are two aspects to every priority: **urgency** and **importance.** For example, assigning a staff member to give a group of schoolchildren a tour of the building has limited business importance. It becomes urgent when the children are standing in the cold while waiting to be invited inside.

The leader's task is to identify these two aspects and then act upon them.

Urgent and important

It takes skill to put decisions into these two categories, a skill that is usually developed through trial and error. There is no golden rulebook to guide a leader to see what is crucial, nor are there right and wrong answers. Over time and with practice, leaders learn to balance urgency with importance.

The main challenge arises when some decisions appear to fit into neither category while others fit both. Also, there are decisions that are only urgent because they have deadlines and provide the basis for future decisions. For example, an organization may want to add an extension to its building and it therefore decides to file a request with the town council. Meeting the council's deadline for this filing has urgency, although the actual building work is scheduled for the next year.

Setting priorities begins by making a list of all the decisions currently under review. To illustrate this, let's imagine that the manager of a ten-person accounts department decides to review all of the upcoming decisions and issues.

He begins by making his list: office decoration, holiday schedules, allocation of staff to new projects and a new health insurance package proposed by the company's personnel office. Each of these decisions includes sub-issues that contribute to making the main decision.

However, the manager wants to avoid getting drawn into the details of each decision before deciding their urgency and importance. His time is particularly tight and so he wants clarity about deadlines as well as an idea about workload so that he can manage day-to-day business and meet future goals.

After the manager lists all the decisions, each can be assessed for urgency and importance. Another list could include all of the sub-issues under each main decision.

List of items	Urgent	Important
Office decoration	No	No
Holiday schedules	Yes	No
Staff project allocation	Yes	Yes
Health insurance	No	Yes

On the list shown here of the main items only, the manager believes that office decoration is neither urgent nor important for the business. Although money is budgeted and there has been much discussion about colours and materials, the proposal originated from their company headquarters 300 miles away.

The staff are enthusiastic, but also happy with their office as it is. This is also the department's busiest season and everyone feels highly pressured by work. The manager decides to send a short email to the person taking charge of this project to ask for an update on progress.

The next item, holiday schedules, is an urgent matter for the short term because people need to make holiday plans with their families. The actual schedule isn't important as long as everyone receives a fair amount of holiday. He decides to send an email to everyone saying that he's posting a holiday sign-up sheet on the office notice board.

Staff allocation for new project work is both urgent and important for the success of the department. The decision is urgent because several projects are just finishing and new assignments must be made to allow people to prepare and make a smooth transition to their new work.

It's also important because skilful scheduling of the right people to the right work directly impacts the department's productivity and therefore its overall budget. The manager likes to meet one to one with staff when each project ends. This gives him an opportunity to ask everyone for their highs and lows on the project and also what they learned. During these meetings, he writes a bullet-point summary for reference during annual reviews and to support future decisions about training.

The decision about health insurance isn't due for weeks, and staff received all the information months ago. However, it's very unlikely that everyone has read this material as yet. They must do this because their decision will lock them into a health plan for an indefinite period. The manager decides to email everyone a reminder using a joke he likes about a doctor attending the wrong patient.

Activity

1 List all the decisions you have to make right now.

2 Identify which are main decisions and which are sub-tasks that contribute to the main decisions.

3 Put a star next to each main decision and then group all of the sub-tasks under each of their main headings.

4 Add another two columns next to the listed items. Label these columns urgent and important.

5 Decide urgency and importance for each item.

6 Make a timeline by drawing a line on a piece of paper and writing the item with the most distant deadline at the bottom of the line, and the item with the most urgent deadline at the top.

7 Next, put any items on the timeline which are important but do not have deadlines. Estimate where they belong relative to the items with deadlines.

8 Finally, put the items that are neither urgent nor important on the line, placing them relative to all the other items.

Drawing a timeline (item 6 in the Activity box) gets things started, but each decision on the list may need further refinement. To illustrate this, the office decoration item can be interpreted in a variety of ways.

For some, it has sub-tasks that include choosing a colour scheme, painting the walls, buying new furniture and creating a layout. For others, the sub-tasks could mean tearing up the floor to upgrade the computer system. So items 1 and 2 in the Activity box need to be clarified.

Clarifying goals

Misunderstandings about goals can disrupt a project at the very start. The office decoration decision is an example. Those in the group who believe that the goal is to improve the office environment will make suggestions that reflect this. Those who think the decision is about upgrading the computer system will neither understand nor be happy with these ideas. There can be much cross-talk and even argument before they all realize that they've interpreted the decision's goal in different ways.

The successful outcome for any decision starts with a **clearly stated goal.** Time is wasted when people lack a shared view of what needs to be done. Alternatively, when goals are clarified, the actions needed to achieve them are undertaken more efficiently.

A goal is a realistic target for achievement. In decision making, it makes explicit the desired end result and the requirements for the decision's success.

The process of setting goals helps decision makers discuss fully what they think should be the end result of the decision. With a shared goal in mind, they can plan a course of action to achieve that goal.

Goals also give decision makers a standard against which they can evaluate their options. They can improve their course of action in order to serve their goal best.

Defining goals

Here are three business situations that require a decision. They each illustrate the importance of how a **goal statement** is phrased:

1 To raise the company's profile
2 To reduce customer complaints by 20 per cent
3 To purchase a two-acre piece of land adjoining the company's headquarters

The **first goal statement** is the most general, and is useful when beginning a decision-making session. It presents a desired end result in general terms and invites people to offer a variety of options. Their options present more specific solutions that can be further discussed.

This discussion helps clarify how each person interprets the idea of raising the company's profile. As a result they can further narrow the focus of their debate. For example, some of the options they generate could include:

- sponsoring a marathon or sports activity
- advertising in a national paper
- getting press coverage for community service projects
- a company executive joining the local school board
- organizing opportunities for executives to speak at conferences or be quoted in the press
- joining professional networking groups.

These six very different options make it obvious that the decision makers have different ideas about what it means to raise the company's profile. So before making a decision about what to do, they have to clarify what they really hope to achieve. For example, do they want to raise their profile nationally or locally? The answer helps them narrow the focus for a second round of suggestions.

The **second goal statement**, to reduce customer complaints by 20 per cent, is more specific. It includes an exact measurement for the decrease. Any option that fails to meet this criterion can be readily eliminated.

When a specific quantity or a precise detail is included in a goal, there should be a good business reason. Details enhance the goal only when they're based on fact and data.

The **third goal statement** is very specific. It limits any options to those that meet all its criteria. This kind of goal is useful when decision makers already know what they need to do. Their task in this case is to generate ideas for how to achieve the goal, rather than to decide what the goal should be.

Stages in the process

The three examples from the previous section show goals that serve decision making at different stages in the process. For example, at the very start it's helpful to have a goal that is phrased in general terms. This invites a variety of options to help the decision makers clarify what needs to be done.

The second style of goal statement is often given to a committee or project team, by bosses, with a mandate to get it done. However, this goal statement usually needs further clarification.

For example, 'customer complaints' might refer to those made to the in-house customer service department, or to blogs, online review sites, social networking sites, or just to the number of items returned after sales. Particularly when this goal statement is non-negotiable and handed ready-formed to decision makers, then it's best to know what it means.

The third style of goal statement usually results after a lot of discussion and hard work about logistical matters of price, timing and legalities. After this goal is identified, however, decision makers may discover that it is impossible to achieve. For example, the landowners may refuse to sell or the price may be too high.

The decision makers must then ask themselves why they wanted that specific piece of land and what else they could do to get the same result without buying that parcel of land. This can open the way to new options they haven't yet considered.

A step-by-step method

There are risks involved in decision making, and the most obvious is making the wrong choice. Decision makers can work to avoid this by using a step-by-step method. Here are the steps:

1 Write a goal statement for the decision.
2 Gather as much information as possible.
3 Generate several options that serve the goal.

4 Ask if the options reveal different interpretations.
5 If so, rephrase the goal statement and repeat step 3.
6 When the goal accurately describes what the decision should achieve, identify at least three options that serve this goal.
7 Test the options using the tally sheets and method described below.
8 Act on the winning option.

Testing the options

Every decision can be met in several ways. That's what creating options is all about. However, when there are several attractive options, it helps if each can be tested against criteria that serve the spirit of the goal. These criteria should be identified just after the goal statement is produced.

There are two levels of criteria: primary requirements and secondary requirements. The **primary requirements** are features that must be satisfied if the goal is to be achieved. **Secondary requirements** support the goal but are not vital.

The crucial difference between primary and secondary requirements is that failure to meet primary requirements will defeat the goal. Primary requirements must be fully met or it is a deal breaker. In contrast, failing to satisfy secondary requirements merely means that the decision is somewhat less suitable, but it still satisfies the goal.

A decision about choosing a holiday illustrates this process. In the following example, a couple has fixed limits for cost, timing and travel method. These are the basis for the holiday's primary requirements. Failure to meet any one of these primary requirements means not having their holiday.

Here are the three primary requirements:

- short travel time – only one work week available
- £2,000 maximum budget for both people
- warm and sunny climate – one person needs the sun to recover from an illness.

In addition, the couple has secondary requirements. These criteria are important to them but not as critical as their primary concerns. Here is a list of their secondary requirements:

- resort on the beach to minimize walking
- travel and hotel package available
- location popular with an age group under 30
- comfortable journey to the hotel
- stable exchange rate
- their native language widely spoken
- sightseeing and night life.

The couple has online information and also brochures for at least 20 resorts. Their goal statement helps them exclude any place featuring adventure sports, educational sightseeing, gourmet dining and a high risk of bad weather. They next list three possible resorts on the tally sheet. Here is a sample of the tally sheet they used:

Goal statement (their desired end result):

Primary requirements	A: Florida World	B: La Plage Splendide	C: Costa Fabula
Short travel time	2 days	1 day	1.5 days
£2,000 maximum budget	£2,500	£1,950	£1,800
Warm and sunny climate	----	yes	yes

They then test their shortlisted resorts against their primary requirements. Both want to go to Florida World, but they have limited holiday time. It would take them a full day of travel to get there – leaving at dawn on a Saturday from a major airport and arriving in Florida late in the evening. Then they would repeat this for their journey home. But they really like the idea and so say, 'Well, maybe,' and write two days in the column.

The next primary requirement refers to cost. Florida World brings them over budget by £500. This is just too much and so reluctantly they decide they have to exclude this option. This means that, even if Florida World meets any further criteria, primary or secondary, it is still off the table.

This illustrates the idea that, if an option fails to meet even one primary requirement, then it is no longer an option.

So the couple looks at La Plage Splendide in France and Costa Fabula in Spain. Both have short journey times. They can reach the French resort from a small airport very near their home, and journey time is about an hour. Total time there and back will be about one day. Costa Fabula is a bit farther from the Spanish airport, but they could still be on the beach by late afternoon of the same day they depart.

Both options are within their budget and also offer sun and dependable weather. Because they meet all their primary requirements, the couple can now test the two options against their list of secondary requirements. They use another tally sheet for this.

After listing their secondary requirements, they score each option, from 1 to 10, against each criterion. This scoring process is subjective and based on how well the couple estimates the option meets the criterion.

The higher the score, the better the option meets the criterion. For example, the French resort has a private beach with cabins, showers and changing rooms on the sand. Costa Fabula's beach is across a road with a narrow strip of sand. So they give Splendide a perfect 10, and Fabula a score of 6.

Secondary requirements	B: La Plage Splendide	C: Costa Fabula
Resort on the beach	10	6
Travel and hotel package	10	7
Location popular with age group	9	8
Comfortable journey to the hotel	10	6
Stable exchange rate	7	7
Native language widely spoken	6	8
Sightseeing and night life	9	6
Total	**61**	**48**

Travel to Splendide is easier than to Fabula and so the couple scores them accordingly. Both are good in terms of appealing to their peer group, but once again Splendide wins because the Costa Fabula draws a slightly younger crowd.

The exchange rate for the Eurozone is reasonably stable, so both options score the same. The Spanish resort features ten languages spoken, while the French hotel says its staff speak English, but it's likely they will prefer to speak only French. However, the French resort has better sightseeing, while the Spanish location offers only a night club scene.

The final score for Splendide is higher than the score for Fabula and so is the clear winner. However, at this stage the couple can review these scores to be sure they consider what is really important to them. They could still decide on Fabula if they identify a new secondary requirement.

What they cannot do is return to Florida World. Once an option fails to meet primary requirements, then it is out. Only if decision makers change or eliminate a primary requirement can an option be returned to the tally. But this means that the changed requirement wasn't really critical and should not have been listed as primary.

This decision-making method forces people to make systematic choices based on known information. It helps avoid wavering and returning to options that are unrealistic and unsuitable.

Activity

- Think of a decision you made today.
- Describe this in one or two sentences.
- Did you have any sense of its priority?
- If so, how did you know this?
- How easily could you distinguish between urgency and long-term importance?
- Did you have a goal or know the outcome you wanted the decision to achieve?
- If you could make the same decision a second time, would you do anything differently?

Summary

Making decisions quickly and implementing them are important leadership skills. It requires identifying priorities and setting goals. However, the best way to improve decision making is actually to make a great many decisions and then evaluate them.

Here is a checklist to help you examine decision-making behaviour on a regular basis:

1 Think about the decisions that you made during the last week. Did you set priorities? Score yourself on your **priority-setting skills** from 1 to 10 (1 = low and 10 = high scoring).

2 Did you use the **step-by-step method**? Score yourself on your use of this method from 1 to 10 (1 = low and 10 = high scoring).

3 Score your ability to identify **primary requirements** (1 = low and 10 = high scoring).

4 Score your ability to identify **secondary requirements** (1 = low and 10 = high scoring).

5 What can you do to improve your decision-making skills overall?

Fact-check (answers at the back)

1. In addition to urgency, what does a priority include?
   a) Importance ❑
   b) Limits ❑
   c) Deadlines ❑
   d) Challenge ❑

2. Which of the following describes a goal?
   a) Primary ❑
   b) Target ❑
   c) Timing ❑
   d) Urgent ❑

3. Which of the following belongs to the step-by-step method?
   a) Intuition ❑
   b) Waiting ❑
   c) Patience ❑
   d) Options ❑

4. What are primary requirements?
   a) Fixed ❑
   b) Standard ❑
   c) Urgent ❑
   d) Long term ❑

5. What are secondary requirements?
   a) Fixed ❑
   b) Absolute ❑
   c) Supportive ❑
   d) Expensive ❑

6. What does a timeline help to manage?
   a) People ❑
   b) Deadlines ❑
   c) Money ❑
   d) Sub-issues ❑

7. Goals help decision makers to do what?
   a) Delay what they need to do ❑
   b) Wonder what they need to do ❑
   c) Hide from what they need to do ❑
   d) Identify what they need to do ❑

8. What do options need to be?
   a) Short term ❑
   b) Fun ❑
   c) Tested ❑
   d) Urgent ❑

9. The scores given to secondary requirements are what?
   a) Subjective ❑
   b) Priorities ❑
   c) Decisions ❑
   d) Basic ❑

10. What gives leaders a way to manage their decisions?
    a) Setting the time ❑
    b) Identifying problems ❑
    c) Setting priorities ❑
    d) Giving orders ❑

LESSON 6

Connecting and linking

Connecting and linking are twenty-first-century skills. They are driven by technology and increasingly are starting points for relationships, both business and social. Leaders need to understand technology and also its uses in order to form networks of colleagues, friends and allies.

In the past, isolation at the top put leaders at risk. Because power and status can intimidate people, leaders can gradually be cut off from those who tell them the truth or challenge their point of view. Now social networking applications alongside widely available Internet links allow leaders to contact supporters directly. The three topics that help leaders make connections are:

- living in a small world
- building trust
- leading at a distance.

Living in a small world

Imagine that each of your friends has at least three contacts that you do not know. Then each of these three new contacts also has three more people that you don't know. This means there are at least 12 people that you don't know but who are connected to you through this single friend. This network of potential contacts is invisible, but real, and is essential to help leaders stay connected to their followers.

Microsoft research

A few years ago, computer scientists at Microsoft Research wanted to know how closely connected people are around the world. Because Microsoft owns Microsoft Messenger, they were able to study all of the instant messages their customers sent. An instant message (IM) is a text message sent 'live' over the Internet. The IM service lets people text back and forth at the same time as each other.

These scientists analysed one month's worth of conversations, which included 30 billion messages among 240 million people. Now, obviously those 240 people do not all know one another. However, the scientists wanted to know how many connections might be shared among all these random strangers. They wondered whether someone in Moscow could be linked to someone in India through friends-of-friends, and not even know it.

For example, Juan Perez in Spain uses IM to contact all his family, friends and work colleagues. Each of these people also knows other people. Some of these friends-of-friends are also connected to some of Juan's existing connections. Juan doesn't know that some of these friends-of-friends exist, and certainly doesn't know they are indirectly connected to him. Juan is in the middle of web of contacts, and so is everyone else using the IM service.

The Microsoft scientists decided to study how many friends-of-friends' connections it takes to link every one of its 240 million IM users to everyone else across their whole network. Surprisingly, this turned out to be just 6.6 connections. (The entire research report can be downloaded free of charge from the Internet. Its web address is in the Further reading and information section under 'Microsoft'.)

Leaders are connected to everyone

The idea that everyone is connected is important for leaders because it means they potentially can reach out to anyone, anywhere. As long as there is one person to link a town, village, community or family, then potentially leaders can contact them by going through just six or seven people.

However, making contact is only a first step. Leaders need *something* more to engage people's attention, and that something is trust. Leaders need to be trustworthy if they want friends-of-friends to listen to them because people follow only those they trust.

Building trust

Trust and emotion

Both honest and dishonest people use similar behaviour to win people's trust. For example, many liars make a show of sincerity by using eye contact, a coaxing tone of voice and open-handed gestures. But so do people who are telling the truth. Ironically, because liars put more effort into the lie, they are often more convincing than honest people.

This is also the case with all kinds of tricksters. They work hard, 24/7, to appear trustworthy and often succeed. This is because decisions about trust are often influenced by emotional reactions. Attractive, charming and seemingly wealthy people are made welcome everywhere because people feel relaxed around them.

The more positive an impression they make (see Lesson 3), the safer people feel in their company. In contrast, someone unwashed, sneering and wearing ragged clothes causes alarm, fear and disgust. These emotional reactions bypass rational thought. Sometimes this reaction is correct, but at other times it isn't.

The trust equation

People make hundreds of mini-decisions during the day, about eating or drinking, completing paperwork or taking exercise. Although the majority of these decisions are unrelated to trust, some are and need a more serious evaluation about whether someone is trustworthy. They need awareness that others are also evaluating them.

This is a challenge, but one made easier as a result of the work of David Maister, Charles Green and Robert Galford. They are all experts on trust and invented the idea of the **trust equation.** Their book, *The Trusted Advisor*, is listed in the Further reading and information section.

The trust equation includes four factors that are the essential ingredients of trust and organizes them into an equation. This can be applied to anyone in any situation. The four factors are:

1 credibility (C)
2 reliability (R)
3 interpersonal, or the degree of closeness between people (I)
4 self-orientation (S).

Note: Maister, Green and Galford use the term 'intimacy' rather than 'interpersonal'. The change here is to support easy understanding among international readers.

The terms defined

C Credibility refers to experience, skills, qualities and credentials.

R Reliability refers to consistent and regular behaviour.

I Interpersonal is the degree of connection felt with this person.

S Self-orientation is the ego and self-service that the person shows.

T Trust is the belief in the delivery of a promised outcome.

Here is the equation:

$$\frac{C + R + I}{S} = T$$

The equation adds the person's credibility, reliability and interpersonal features (C+R+I) as the numerator or top number of the equation. Then it divides this total by the degree of self-orientation (S), the denominator or bottom number. The result is the person's trustworthiness.

For example, if the person being evaluated has a high degree of credibility, is reliable and is well known to the evaluator, then the sum of these three factors will be high (C+R+I). However, the evaluator also needs to consider whether the person is self-serving. If the score for S is high, then dividing this into the (C+R+I) number produces a low trust score. Here are two problems that show how to apply the trust equation to work situations.

Problem 1

Marie has all the qualifications necessary to lead a project team and has also led similar teams in her previous job. You know that she keeps her promises and stays late to ensure that deadlines are met. You also know her well because she's been open about her family background and interests. This combination means her score for C+R+I is high. As for her self-orientation, Marie is ambitious and makes it clear that she wants a promotion when the right opportunity arises. However, she's a loyal employee. If she leads the team, she serves the company as well as her own career goals. So she gets a low score for self-orientation. Her equation looks like this:

$$\frac{C + R + I}{S} = T \qquad \frac{\text{High}}{\text{Low}} = \text{High trust}$$

Problem 2

Egele is very good at his job. Although he's worked on project teams for five years, he's never been the leader. He is seen to be a risky choice because he disappears for days to work alone when he feels under stress. This leaves his team mates guessing and often unable to finish their work until he reappears. Egele also rarely converses with his colleagues. His response to complaints about his behaviour is just to look away. This combination means his score for C+R+I is very low. As for self-orientation, last year he told a colleague that he was so angry at the company that he thought about sabotaging the project's results. This gives him a high S score. His trust equation looks like this:

$$\frac{C + R + I}{S} = T \qquad \frac{Low}{High} = Low\ trust$$

Adding numbers

The originators of the trust equation, Maister, Green and Galford, also suggested quantifying it – that is, giving a numerical estimate for each of the four factors. These numbers would be based on a subjective assessment of the person. For example, before the boss decides who should assume project leadership, he or she should identify, in advance, the criteria for a top score of 10, and also for a bottom score of 1.

This step helps clarify the standards for project leadership, and should be done for each factor: credibility, reliability, interpersonal and self-orientation. He or she would then score each person wanting the job against these criteria by estimating where they are between scores of 1 and 10. When there are several people wanting the job, a numerical scoring process can improve fairness.

Leading at a distance

Many businesses now depend on smart technology to connect co-workers. This both encourages growth and minimizes costs. However, the increased dependency on technology has an impact on trust. For example, in face-to-face work situations, people see their colleagues' behaviour directly and decide to trust them based on this experience.

When direct contact is removed, people need additional opportunities to experience their colleagues' behaviour in order to support development of mutual trust. Research shows that regular communication, using several methods simultaneously, increases trust among colleagues who work at a distance from each other. Methods can include:

- email
- video telephoning such as Skype
- Twitter – or a clone of this service
- blogging
- an in-house clone of Facebook
- instant messaging or text messages.

In fact, any communication method that helps people learn more about each other will increase their opportunity to connect, bond and form links. Communication supports the I-factor (interpersonal) in the trust equation. Leaders who ask colleagues to work together at a distance also need to offer new ways for them to connect easily.

The table below shows the relationship between eight technology-driven communication methods and the four trust equation factors. Each method supports the equation factors in different ways. For example, people who answer their email immediately can seem reliable. A blog offers opportunities to share candid opinions and therefore helps readers feel as if they know the blogger well. A Facebook clone or social website, organized by the leader, gives co-workers a 'show and tell' opportunity. This can have an effect on credibility.

Technology-driven communication methods

Email means 'electronic mail' and is sent using digital technology.

Skype clone means a software application that allows audio and video calls using digital technology over the Internet.

Blog is an abbreviation of 'web log' and is a website that presents the opinions of the web logger as well as multimedia offerings.

SMS means 'short messaging service' and is text-based using a phone.

MMS means a 'multimedia messaging service' and includes photo, video and audio sent using a phone.

IM means 'instant messaging' and is live, text-based exchanges by two or more people using digital technology over the Internet.

Twitter clone refers to a burst of information sent as a text message over the Internet that uses no more than 140 characters.

Facebook clone means a website that allows people to post information about themselves so that others can access this, learn about them and hear their news.

The relationship between technology-driven communication methods and the four trust equation factors

	Credibility	Reliability	Interpersonal	Self-orientation
Email				
Skype clone				
Blog				
SMS				
MMS				
IM				
Twitter clone				
Facebook clone				

Activity

1 Identify how each communication method supports each of the four equation factors.

2 Choose one networking method from this list that you have never used before. If you've used them all, then choose the one you use least often.

3 Go online and learn more about the method you chose.

4 Identify three benefits to your leadership performance that this method could bring.

5 Experiment with this method; that is, set up an account on a website offering this as a free service, then try the method.

6 Make sure your efforts include a blog or Twitter account.

7 Ask colleagues and friends for their reactions to your efforts.

Summary

This lesson focused on the skills leaders need to bring people together. Of critical importance is their need to be both trustworthy themselves and also to build trust among their colleagues. This becomes more challenging when colleagues work at a distance because people usually depend upon their own senses to decide whom to trust.

Multiple communication methods can act as a substitute for face-to-face contact. Leaders should use these methods frequently and encourage everyone else to participate. The reward for this effort is a well-functioning team.

Here is a checklist to help you assess and improve your colleagues' and your own trustworthiness:

1 Apply the trust equation to each of your co-workers.

2 Whom do you trust and why? Are there any surprises?

3 Is it possible to improve your own trust score:
(a) when making new contacts?
(b) among the people who already know you?

4 How can you support other people to improve their scores?

5 Are you using all the technology available to you to improve communication?

6 If not, how can you increase both the quantity and quality of your communication?

Fact-check (answers at the back)

1. How many links did it take for everyone using Microsoft's instant messaging service to be connected to everyone else?
   a) 10.9 ❏
   b) 108 ❏
   c) 6.6 ❏
   d) 28 ❏

2. Microsoft Research studied how many messages?
   a) 42 million ❏
   b) 2 billion ❏
   c) 30 billion ❏
   d) 260 million ❏

3. Which of the following is a factor in the trust equation?
   a) Reliability ❏
   b) Awareness ❏
   c) Honesty ❏
   d) Friendship ❏

4. A trust equation like this would have what kind of score?

   $$\frac{Low\ C + R + I}{High\ S}$$

   a) High trust ❏
   b) Low trust ❏
   c) Mid trust ❏
   d) Outer trust ❏

5. A trust equation like this would have which score?

   $$\frac{High\ C + R + I}{Low\ S}$$

   a) High trust ❏
   b) Low trust ❏
   c) Mid trust ❏
   d) Outer trust ❏

6. When face-to-face contact decreases, what must increase?
   a) Travel ❏
   b) Marketing ❏
   c) Salaries ❏
   d) Communication ❏

7. Credibility refers to experience, qualities credentials and what?
   a) Banking ❏
   b) Skills ❏
   c) References ❏
   d) Honesty ❏

8. What does self-orientation refer to?
   a) Confidence ❏
   b) Knowledge ❏
   c) Mapping ❏
   d) Egotism ❏

9. What does reliability refer to?
   a) Consistency ❏
   b) Promises ❏
   c) Pacing ❏
   d) Timing ❏

10. Interpersonal refers to the degree of what felt with another person?
    a) Psychology ❏
    b) Staffing ❏
    c) Distance ❏
    d) Connection ❏

LESSON 7

Vision and inspiration

Vision inspires action and brings people together. Research shows that vision can even be a more effective motivator than cash, bonuses or prized office space.

Vision is like having a light in the distance to guide the way and give direction. When this light is clear and bright, a leader can describe it vividly and well, and so it easily attracts attention, curiosity and interest.

Leaders need to understand and work with vision so that they can inspire others. The topics that support this understanding include:

- meaning and purpose
- seeing the big picture
- the skills of framing and reframing.

Meaning and purpose

Leaders with **vision** remind people that there is more to life than the routine and the ordinary. Vision offers them a common purpose that everyone can achieve together. In general, however, visionaries are not the most comfortable kind of people to be around.

Particularly when their ideas differ from conventional or mainstream points of view, visionaries are often judged by the world to be fanatics, freaks or 'nutters'. Extreme thinking is too unusual for widespread acceptance, and frequently the determined visionary contributes to this negative reaction by behaving in an eccentric way.

However, it's vision, not the behaviour of visionaries, which transforms an ordinary manager or administrator into a leader. Vision suggests that it is possible to make things better and this is inspiring. Here is the definition of leadership that appeared at the beginning of this development programme:

> *'Leadership is the ability to present a vision so that others want to achieve it. Leaders need the skill to work with other people as well as the belief that they can make a difference.'*

Managers and administrators, in contrast to leaders, present ideas, proposals, memos and suggestions. They ask, insist, direct, demand, suggest, convince and encourage their colleagues to co-operate. Depending on their degree of authority and influence, they can also be assured of success. While effective management deserves both praise and reward, it is not leadership.

Leaders have vision, take risks, present dreams, explore possibilities and in general invite their colleagues to join them for a journey to the unknown. Managers write reports, analyse data and ask their colleagues to meet them in the conference room after lunch. Even when leaders blend well into their organizational surroundings, there is something different about them. On close examination, that something is vision.

Whenever individuals lift their attention above routine matters, they open themselves to new possibilities. The ability to imagine something new and better can be acquired with practice. The necessary effort is worthwhile because vision is an essential part of leadership. The next activity is designed to improve your sense of vision.

Activity

1 Ask yourself if there is someone you admire whose point of view surprises you or makes you think. You can choose anyone, including a public figure or someone you actually know.

- What quality or qualities do you imagine inspires their point of view?

2 Remember a time when you've seen this person show this quality in action.

- Can you imagine showing this quality yourself?

3 When you next make plans for your future, take a minute to ask whether you can use this quality while planning.

- Let yourself wonder whether your future plans would improve if you used this quality or whether the person you admire could be there to advise you.

It has already been suggested that people who have vision aren't always comfortable people. They are also often unpopular. The decision to be a leader instead of an effective manager should not be taken lightly. The front line is far more dangerous than the back, and the challenges of leadership are far greater than those of supervision or administration.

Leadership requires a high level of commitment and the loss of much personal choice. The glamour of having vision won't soften the blow if that vision is rejected or is widely misunderstood. This experience is far more painful for a leader than the rejection of a proposal or working paper can be for a manager.

Leaders, by definition, have the kind of relationship with their followers that makes them more vulnerable to their reactions. However tough or macho some leaders may appear, it is hard for them to avoid feeling hurt when their most deeply felt ideas are rejected.

It helps when leaders feel confident that they are the right person for their position. They can also draw on their sense of vision to sustain them when or if they have a difficult time convincing others that their vision is worthwhile. Vision may create vulnerability, but it also supports inner strength when under fire.

Seeing the big picture

'Seeing the big picture' is a phrase often used to describe the act of shifting attention from the details of a situation to see how all the details fit together to make a whole. The big picture integrates all of the details into a coherent image, like seeing that there is a forest rather than a group of single and separate trees. Seeing the big picture is like taking a mental step back to absorb more information. This is an antidote to becoming stuck in petty issues or daily routine.

The purpose of looking at the big picture is to explore the meaning of an existing situation. Leaders who want to see the big picture should first focus very hard on the details of a situation so that each item becomes separate.

Then they should clear their mind and think about the situation again. This time they want to look for a pattern or a picture that ignores specific details. This act of shifting perspective can be shown with an optical illusion:

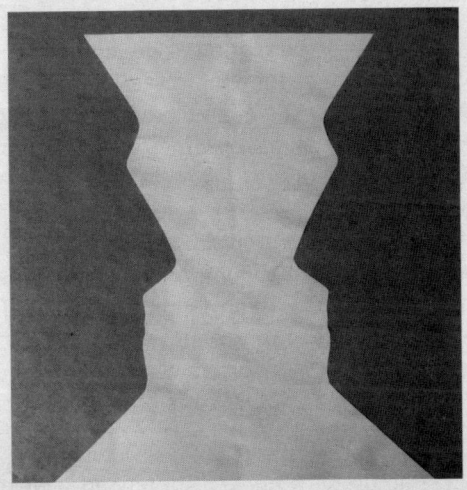

An optical illusion is a trick the eye plays so that a picture can look very different from changing points of view. Looking for the big picture in a situation can be like seeing an optical illusion.

To demonstrate this, focus your gaze on the centre of the picture. Very likely the image of a vase appears. Next, shift your attention to the right side of the picture. Then slowly move your eyes to the middle. A profile of a face is now likely to appear. Then shift your attention to the left side of the picture and move your eye towards the centre. A second profile should emerge.

Just as this picture can be 'read' in two ways, events can change appearance and meaning depending upon point of view. The broader the point of view that leaders take, the more likely they are to include the necessary information to interpret events correctly. They can also gain a fresh perspective and often find solutions to nagging problems. Seeing the big picture allows new patterns to emerge and can create a better understanding about working relationships, circumstances or events.

Artificial divisions can fall away when people and events are seen in a wider context. Sometimes this is called **helicopter viewing** – that is, leaders mentally raise their point of view to look at what is happening as if from above. This can reveal a story that may otherwise be hidden or difficult to see.

On occasion, big-picture thinking reveals hidden threats. In this case, the leader may see a big picture that includes the whole marketplace with allies, enemies and potential business opportunities. This can support action taking before serious difficulties arise.

Courage in the face of adversity is an inspiring leadership quality. Like the hero in an action film, the leader must always believe in the possibility of a happy ending, even if there seems only the remotest chance of this. A leader's core task is to show the way forward in an inspiring way regardless of conflict, problem or challenge. Seeing the big picture helps achieve this.

> **Activity**
>
> 1 Watch an exchange between two people that you don't know.
>
> 2 Make guesses about this exchange in terms of (a) the purpose of their contact, (b) the underlying emotions they may feel, both positive and negative, and (c) the expressed emotion they both show, both positive and negative.
>
> 3 Now focus on just one of the people. Imagine (a) how they got to the meeting, (b) what connection that person has to the other, and (c) where they will go after the meeting.

Shifting perspective like this, on demand, is a core skill for seeing the big picture and is useful to practise.

Framing and reframing

Framing

The dictionary defines framing as 'an established order or system, or the way that a thing may be constructed, organized or formed'. A frame can also be described as the habits of mind that people follow when they interpret what is happening around them. Lesson 3 raised the idea of bias as a mental habit. It is also an example of a frame.

Every single person has a unique **frame of reference.** That's why people can describe the same event seen at the same time in different ways. For example, one person may notice a red jacket because he owns one just like it. Another viewer may see people smiling because she is happy that day herself. Past experience, personal values, attitudes and states of mind influence what viewers choose to look at in a scene.

However, like any other habit, frames can be changed. This takes time, effort and commitment, but is necessary when frames of reference create negative ways of thinking and may stop a leader from doing well.

Reframing

The process of changing a frame of reference or mental habit is called reframing. By definition, this is changing perspective in order to gain new insight and to discover whether any information has been misunderstood. Reframing is consciously choosing to see the world in a new way.

A reframe creates an entirely new story about what is seen, and intentionally interprets information in a different way from usual. The purpose is to break old habits, bias and rigid ideas. By challenging their own points of view, leaders can discover new possibilities.

This is useful when people believe they are stuck. Leaders can feel as if they have no options or are trapped into making only predetermined choices. If those choices are all unattractive, then leaders need to shake themselves up and force themselves to see the world with new eyes.

This skill helps leaders because it creates mental flexibility. It also supports development of vision. Why? Because when people are locked in a single way of seeing the world, they reduce their capacity to invent new things. For them, the distant light on the hill will always be just another all-night petrol station.

Reframing allows new outcomes to emerge. Leaders need the zest that a truly open mind allows them to experience. When they see that light on a distant hill, they think big thoughts and aspire to new things. This is one step beyond the big picture.

Seeing the big picture is a good first step when seeking a new point of view. However, on occasion, when leaders are so caught in routine, this yields nothing. The next step is to reframe what is happening and what is being seen.

Why reframe?

Although the facts of a situation may be indisputable, the frame of reference that each observer uses to interpret those facts differs with each person.

To illustrate this, look at the example of three friends who meet at the end of every week in the coffee room to talk about their weekend plans.

- The boss sees this and thinks: 'Those three are always wasting time.'
- The shy and lonely file clerk looks at them and thinks sadly, 'Those three are such good friends. I wish I could join them, but they would just ignore me.'
- The office busybody sees their meeting as a chance to ask them to help move some furniture.

Based on their different frames of reference, each person interprets the same group of three friends in very different ways. They see what they see through emotional bias. To the extent that each of these three viewers has a rigid bias or mental frame, they limit their opportunity to see things differently.

Reframing gets a leader to choose a different emotional reaction to what is seen or, alternatively, to interpret it differently. Further, reframers do this on purpose and on demand, fully aware that this changes their reactions. For example, the boss in the example above could remember that it is their coffee break and so they can talk about anything they wish. He could also follow his doctor's advice and 'lighten up' and be 'less critical'.

The shy person could recognize that the three people are the most popular people in the office and so decide to study them. Are there any stories they tell or ways of laughing, sitting and being relaxed that make them appear so attractive? If the shy person wishes, this can be a wake-up call. Why not copy them? Why not assume a different attitude towards life?

How to reframe

This activity presents a way to practise reframing:

> **Activity**
>
> 1 Choose a magazine or journal. Look through it until you find a picture with people who capture your attention.
>
> - Without reading an explanation of the picture, interpret what you see. This interpretation is your **original frame.**
>
> 2 Now look at the picture again and choose to interpret the picture in a completely different way.
>
> - To do this, imagine...
>   - there is a different emotional atmosphere from the one you first believed you saw
>   - that the people you see have different motives and intentions from those you first thought
>   - that the centre of power is changed so that the people who, at first, you thought were less powerful are now the dominant ones.
> - This new interpretation is your **reframe.** You can repeat this process whenever you need new insight.

Summary

Presenting a vision is the hardest leadership skill to develop, but it yields a great reward. Vision opens the way to possibility and invites people to feel inspired to create new opportunities.

The following checklist reviews the balance between envisioning new solutions and managing people and resources. The more senior a leader's role, the more time should be spent on using vision to plan for the future and find new solutions.

1. Do you spend all your working time on administration or supervision?

2. Do you give yourself time to imagine new solutions or ideas?

3. How often do you invite your colleagues to think of new solutions or offer new ideas?

4. Do you try to shift your perspective from a narrow field to include a bigger picture?

5. If so, what goes well with this? If not, can you try to frame and reframe for this situation?

6. What do you like and not like about your effort to reframe?

7. How can you improve your reframing skills in future?

Fact-check (answers at the back)

1. Which of the following best relates to 'vision'?
a) Money ❑
b) Dreams ❑
c) Reports ❑
d) Managers ❑

2. What does 'the big picture' mean?
a) A map ❑
b) A movie ❑
c) An oil painting ❑
d) The whole ❑

3. What does reframing mean?
a) Opinions ❑
b) A survey ❑
c) Shifting views ❑
d) Optimism ❑

4. Why do leaders need vision?
a) To inspire people ❑
b) To frighten people ❑
c) To manage people ❑
d) To control people ❑

5. Which of the following describes an optical illusion?
a) Myopia ❑
b) Glasses ❑
c) Trick ❑
d) Video ❑

6. What kind of reaction does a reframe change?
a) An unexpected one ❑
b) An emotional one ❑
c) An open one ❑
d) An interesting one ❑

7. A frame is a mental what?
a) Problem ❑
b) Issue ❑
c) Dream ❑
d) Habit ❑

8. Vision can make leaders what?
a) Carefree ❑
b) Truthful ❑
c) Unpopular ❑
d) Lazy ❑

9. What can big-picture thinking reveal?
a) Hidden threats ❑
b) Hidden rooms ❑
c) Hidden ideas ❑
d) Hidden people ❑

10. What don't managers need?
a) Power ❑
b) Direction ❑
c) Vision ❑
d) Money ❑

7 × 7

1 Seven key ideas

- **Know yourself.** Self-awareness is a leadership essential. You need to know why you do what you do before you can understand what motivates others.
- **Control your impulses.** Angry, impulsive reactions to people and events waste time and energy. Think things through and manage your behaviour wisely.
- **Look and listen.** Look at people and listen when they speak to you, and pay attention to their whole story, gestures, words and facial expression. This creates understanding.
- **Clear thinking allows clear speaking.** Organize your thoughts before explaining or giving directions. Use simple language, bullet points and short sentences to describe what is needed and by what deadline.
- **Tolerate differences.** Fully accept that other people's choices and priorities are important to them, even if you think they are wrong. Begin a discussion with respect for different points of view and truly listen.
- **Build relationships.** Leaders work through others and so relationships with people above, below and sideways are all equally important.
- **Delegate.** Identify what you need to do yourself and what could and should be done by others. This frees your time to innovate and solve problems.

2 Seven of the best resources

- **Cialdini, Robert**, *Influence: the Psychology of Persuasion* (Harper, 2006). Selling over two million copies and translated into 16 languages, this book offers six principles explaining how influence works.
- **Galford, Robert and Drapeau, Anne Seibold**, *The Trusted Leader* (The Free Press, 2011). Trust supports relationships.

This book explains how to gain trust and assess better when to trust others.
- **Goleman, Daniel**, 'Leadership that gets results' (*Harvard Business Review*, March–April 2000). This article presents six leadership styles and how they influence profits.
- **Leadership testing online.** This website offers free access to personality testing, including a Leadership Test, a Situational Judgement Test and an Interpersonal Skills Test. www.psychometrictest.org.uk/
- **MacGregor Burns, James**, *Leadership* (Harper, 2012). This is a classic and essential for anyone who wants to understand modern leadership. First published in 1978, it explains that leaders and followers depend on each other. His ideas are widely copied all over the world.
- **Mind Tools.** This website is a general resource for ideas about leadership, with blog entries from experts advising how to lead better. www.mindtools.com/pages/article/newLDR_83.htm
- **Weeks, Holly**, *Failure to Communicate: How Conversations Go Wrong and What You Can Do To Right Them* (Harvard Business Press, 2010). Difficult conversations cause stress and jangle nerves. This book serves as a reference for leaders from every profession everywhere.

3 Seven things to avoid

- **Hesitation.** Once you decide, take action. Opportunities are lost when you let doubt take over.
- **Rushing people, ideas, decisions or yourself.** This leads to mistakes and repeated effort. Take time to think things through, decide and then act.
- **Narrow thinking.** Believing that your opinion is the only one that matters is a mistake. This blocks not only your own creativity but other people's as well.
- **Talking too much.** This stops anyone else from sharing ideas and finding solutions. When one person dominates a conversation, this also demotivates everyone else.

- **Stress.** The chemicals surging into your blood with stress damage health and cloud your judgement. Take breaks to recharge. Enjoy a joke. Eat well and be healthy.
- **Confused goals and poor planning.** Leaders are responsible for more than their own success. They need to plan effectively to get the most from shared resources. This means clear goals and getting buy-in to plans.
- **Discourtesy of any kind to anyone.** 'Please', 'Thank you' and 'You're welcome' are key words for leaders. Smiling, waiting your turn and showing respect are key behaviours.

4 Seven inspiring leaders

- **Nelson Mandela.** He faced terrible injustice with resilience, patience and strength. His self-awareness enabled him to rise above hardship and show compassion and tolerance to others.
- **Eleanor Roosevelt.** She led the formation of the United Nations and chaired the commission that drafted and approved the Universal Declaration of Human Rights.
- **Mahatma Gandhi.** He was committed to non-violent and peaceful protest. His inner authority and belief in a just cause drew international attention to India's independence movement.
- **Angela Merkel.** This three-term leader of Germany is widely respected for her judgement and strength of character. She is a decisive and strong world leader.
- **Sir Tim Berners-Lee.** He invented the World Wide Web, not just the idea of global access to information for everyone, but also the computer language that made this happen. Of greater importance, however, is his decision that all access should be free to all.
- **Aung San Suu Kyi.** A Burmese leader who endured 15 years of house arrest, she demonstrated the power of peaceful resistance and brought about social and political change through her writing and example.
- **Steve Jobs.** His name is synonymous with innovation, vision and life-changing products that are both beautiful and functional.

5 Seven great quotes

- 'In any moment of decision, the best thing you can do is the right thing, the next best thing is the wrong thing, and the worst thing you can do is nothing.' Theodore Roosevelt
- 'The single biggest problem with communication is the illusion that it has taken place.' George Bernard Shaw
- 'At one time leadership meant muscle; but today it means getting along with people.' Indira Gandhi
- 'Your time is limited, so don't waste it living someone else's life. Don't be trapped by dogma – which is living with the results of other people's thinking. Don't let the noise of others' opinions drown out your own inner voice. And most important, have the courage to follow your heart and intuition.' Steve Jobs
- 'Trust yourself. Create the kind of self that you will be happy to live with all your life. Make the most of yourself by fanning the tiny, inner sparks of possibility into flames of achievement.' Golda Meir
- 'Excellence is never an accident. It is always the result of high intention, sincere effort, and intelligent execution.' Aristotle
- 'Courage is the most important of all the virtues, because without courage you can't practise any other virtue consistently. You can practise any virtue erratically, but nothing consistently without courage.' Maya Angelou

6 Seven things to do today

- Contact a former colleague that you once knew well – just to say hello.
- Set aside 15 minutes to be alone to think about what you want in your life in five years' time.
- Identify one beneficial project and develop a goal statement for it as well as its primary and secondary requirements.
- At the end of the day, score yourself for self-awareness during the day, giving a 5 for 'excellent' and a 1 for 'didn't try'. Do this every day for the next week.

- Choose someone you believe communicates well. Watch him or her in conversation and identify something to copy.
- At the start of the day, think of your least favourite activity. Decide what you can add or subtract from it to feel more motivated about doing it.
- As you go through the day, think about the kind of power you are using for each activity. Ask if it is the best choice and consider alternatives.

7 Seven trends for tomorrow

- **Social media strategy**: social media will continue to grow and demand your time. Find a balance so that you feel part of things, but are also independent and able to turn off when you like.
- **Personal branding**: the workplace is growing more fluid and you need a single unified message about who you are and what you have to offer. This is the brand you bring with you when changing roles and jobs.
- **The sharing economy**: the move to shared ownership will gather speed with even greater cloud access to images and ideas, along with multi-user cars, bicycles, homes and even garden tools.
- **Diversity**: migration from south to north will increase as more people struggle to gain a foothold in richer European countries. Be prepared to accept and understand differences as the social map continues to change.
- **Social responsibility**: this is an age of social awareness and community responsibility. Leaders need to think beyond their immediate personal interest.
- **The Internet of things**: smart technology connecting ordinary objects means more automation and greater freedom for more fulfilling work and social activity.
- **Big data**: this trend is both a challenge and major social benefit. Through the deluge of information, people everywhere can access data from global sources. This transforms lives.

Further reading and information

Dunbar, Robin, *How Many Friends Does One Person Need?* (Faber, 2011)

Ferrucci, Piero, *What We May Be* (Penguin, 2009)

Galford, Robert and Drapeau, Anne, *The Trusted Leader* (The Free Press, 2002)

Leskovec, Jure and Horvitz, Eric, *Planetary-scale Views on an Instant-messaging Network*, available online at http://arxiv.org/abs/0803.0939 (2008)

Maister, David, Green, Charles and Galford, Robert, *The Trusted Advisor* (The Free Press, 2001)

MacGregor Burns, James, *Leadership* (Harper Perennial Political Classics, 2010)

Maslow, Abraham, *Motivation and Personality*, 3rd edn (Addison-Wesley, 1987)

Maslow, Abraham: official publications website for all of Dr Maslow's books and audio at www.maslow.com

Microsoft Research: Refer to Leskovec, Jure (above), and Sanderson, Katherine (below)

O'Connor, Carol, website: www.visiprac.com or email: carol@visiprac.com

Sanderson, Katherine, *Six Degrees of Messaging*, available at http://www.nature.com/news/2008/080313/full/news.2008.670.html

TED Lectures, available at www.ted.com: an online collection of video-recorded lectures given by leaders in their field

Answers

Lesson 1: 1c; 2d; 3b; 4a; 5b; 6c; 7a; 8b; 9d; 10a.
Lesson 2: 1a; 2c; 3b; 4d; 5b; 6a; 7c; 8b; 9d; 10a.
Lesson 3: 1a; 2d; 3c; 4d; 5a; 6b; 7c; 8b; 9d; 10a.
Lesson 4: 1b; 2a; 3b; 4d; 5c; 6a; 7d; 8b; 9c; 10a.

Lesson 5: 1a; 2b; 3d; 4a; 5c; 6b; 7d; 8c; 9a; 10c.
Lesson 6: 1c; 2c; 3a; 4b; 5a; 6d; 7b; 8d; 9a; 10d.
Lesson 7: 1b; 2d; 3c; 4a; 5c; 6b; 7d; 8c; 9a; 10c.

About the author

Dr Carol O'Connor has more than 30 years' experience teaching leadership. She's worked on five continents for businesses, governments, charities and professional firms with people from every level of management. She believes that anyone can be a leader as long as there is the willingness to step up and take responsibility on the day.